Richard & Judy's Winning Stories

First published in Great Britain in 2003 by
Chrysalis Children's Books, an imprint of Chrysalis Books Group
The Chrysalis Building
Bramley Road
London W10 6SP
www.chrysalisbooks.co.uk

A CIP catalogue record for this book is available from the British Library.

ISBN 1 8445 020 2

Set in Bembo and Daddy O
Printed and bound in Great Britain
by Mackays of Chatham plc

2 4 6 8 10 9 7 5 3 1

This book can be ordered direct from the publisher. Please contact the Marketing Department. But try your bookshop first.

RICHARD & JUDY'S WINNING STORIES

CHRYSALIS CHILDREN'S BOOKS

Acknowledgements

Richard and Judy would like to thank Eoin Colfer, Gillian Cross, Anne Fine, Terry Jones, Michael Morpurgo, Kate Petty and Ruth Symes for their advice to the viewers, and to thank Liz Flanagan, George Gray, Anthony Horowitz, Lynne Reid Banks, Amanda Ross and Ruth Symes for judging the competition.

Contents

Winning story!

Foreword

Children's literature has always been very close to both of our hearts. We both loved reading as kids – Judy's mother used to despair about the amount of time she spent with her head in a book!

Books provide a way of escaping reality and venturing boldly into worlds where anything can happen and there is no better example of this than children's literature.

Great children's writing isn't just for children. As Terry Jones said on our show, the first rule of writing for children is "Don't". If you write condescendingly for kids they will know and they won't read your books or listen to your stories.

A writer who knows this better than any other is JK Rowling who, with her Harry Potter saga, not only introduced millions of children to the joys of reading but also captivated millions of adults too (ourselves included).

Naturally, we have very different tastes. As a child, Richard was gripped by *Treasure Island* and Sherlock Holmes, while Judy was hooked by Angela Brazil's *Chalet School* series and also loved the classics *Little Women* and *Jane Eyre*. This collection reflects the same kind of diversity.

When we launched this competition we were astounded by the response. Our viewers really are a creative and talented lot. The difficulty wasn't finding twenty-five entries good enough for inclusion in this book; it was whittling down the thousands of wonderful entries to only twenty-five and we are both very proud to be involved in this project.

Well enough of us, if you're sitting comfortably… Once upon a time…

Henry's Cage

Winning story!

Graham Denney

I have come to the conclusion that it is impossible to sleep with one eye open. 'I'll be sleeping with one eye open' is a much-used saying – the idea being that if you are scared of something bad happening to you while you sleep, you can keep one eye open to look out for any danger.

This, of course, is nonsense. You cannot do both things at once. If you fall asleep, your eyes will close. If you want to keep one eye open, you will have to stay awake. Spending your nights in such a manner is not 'sleeping with one eye open', it is 'being awake with one eye shut'.

'Being awake with one eye shut' is, however, definitely possible, and I have found that it can be useful in many situations, such as being outside on a very sunny day, preparing for a winking context, or pretending to be a pirate.

Here, then, is a rather scary story that involves 'being awake with one eye shut'.

Iris Ventolin squirmed sleepily against her seatbelt

and wrestled herself over on to her side. Time to swap eyes; left's turn now.

It had been a very long car ride to Grandad's and Iris was trying desperately hard not to fall asleep. For the last hour, she had been staying awake with one eye shut, swapping every five minutes between her left eye and her right to give them each a little rest without ever dozing off completely. It was good idea because, as everybody knows, it is impossible to fall asleep with one eye open.

But, it hadn't been easy for Iris to stay awake. It hadn't helped that her mother and father hadn't said a word for the last forty minutes. It hadn't helped that the radio was too quiet to be heard from the back seat. And it hadn't helped that out here in these wooded country lanes the night was impossibly dark, and the only thing to see out of the window was the never-ending thatch of dead white trees in the headlights.

Iris wobbled her loose front tooth idly back and forth with the tip of her tongue. Gradually, she let her left eye droop to match her right, and nuzzled her hot face into the padding of the seat.

Suddenly, Iris's father slammed his foot on the brakes and the car lurched forward. Iris woke with a start and looked up in time to see an extraordinarily tall, spaghetti-haired old man in a moth-eaten blue raincoat run out into the road ahead, chasing after a terrified wild rabbit.

Fortunately, the car had excellent brakes and steering and, with a simple swerve, Iris's father was able to avoid hitting the old man. Without stopping, they drove round him and on down the road.

'What an idiot!' cried her mother, looking back over her shoulder. Iris's father fixed his eyes on the road ahead, gripped the steering-wheel tightly and said nothing.

The rabbit scampered away into the trees. Iris had felt the old man's desperate, shark-black eyes following her as they passed, and she turned to watch him out of the rear window as they drove away. By the red glow of the tail-lights she saw him beginning to lope after the car on his dreadful bony legs. . .

★

'I'm telling you, it was him! It was Henry Shade!' whispered Iris's father anxiously.

'Maybe it was, but it's nothing to worry about,' said Grandad calmly. 'He doesn't come here any more. Nobody's seen him in the village for years.'

'Your father's right, Jack. Did you see the way he was wheezing when he ran after the car? I doubt he could have made it to the end of the road, let alone all the way down to the village,' added Iris's mother reassuringly.

'Well, maybe you're right. . .' shrugged Iris's father.

Iris lay on the sofa, listening to the grown-ups. She had fallen asleep in the car, but had secretly woken up when her father had carried her into the house.

Nobody knew that, rather than being asleep, she was actually awake with both eyes shut, and could hear everything that they were saying.

Later, when Grandad was tucking her into bed and Inky the cat had kneaded out a nice comfy sleeping place at her side, Iris opened her eyes and asked, 'Who's Henry Shade?'

'Ah,' said Grandad, sitting down on the bed beside her and scratching the nape of his neck. 'Someone's been listening in, then. Been sleeping with one ear open, have you? That Henry Shade's just a funny old man who lives out in the woods,' said Grandad, soothingly. 'Don't you worry about him.'

'*Why* does he live in the woods? Why was he chasing that rabbit?' asked Iris, sitting up. 'I'm not going to sleep until you tell me all about him,' she added, crossing her arms to prove her intent. Grandad looked hesitantly towards the bedroom door to check that no one was listening, licked his lips, and leaned in close. Iris knew that he could never resist the chance to tell a story.

'Well, if you insist,' he whispered with an eager grin. 'It *is* a good story.'

Grandad stroked at his big thick eyebrows with his fingertip and sucked deliciously on his dentures.

'So, Henry of the Morning Shade. . . Where shall I start?'

So, Grandad told the story of Henry Shade. I shall sum it up for you, because Grandad tends to ramble on a bit when you ask him a question. I certainly won't bother telling you where he eventually did start his story because it was teeth-grindingly irrelevant.

Also, the child I am having type out this story for me has to start cooking my dinner soon, so I don't want to keep him chained to the typewriter for too much longer.

Here, then, are the important parts:

Out in the woods on the edge of the village lives a thirteen-foot tall, moth-eaten old man called Henry Shade. The locals believe that he has been in this woods for centuries. There's even an old rhyme about him:

In the woods beyond the village,
Where strange things' homes are made,
Lives the loathsome, lanky, lungless old man
That folk call Henry Shade.

He'll be coming a-lurking 'fore dawn
Looking to snatch and to thieve
The beasts from your yard and your hearth
And steal off the air that they breathe.

So lock up your barns good and tight,
And bolt all your windows and doors.

And sleep with one eye open in case,
The next house he calls on is yours . . .

Years ago, Henry would creep out of the woods and down to the village. He would come in the early hours of the morning, in the half-light before dawn. He stalked the streets and yards looking for animals left out at night, and he would go back and forth, scratching and rattling at windows and doors, trying to find ways into people's houses to steal their pets.

What did he do with the animals? Well, you see . . .

. . . *Henry Shade has no lungs.*

That's right. He has no lungs, no ribs – not even a proper chest. He has only a cage, like a big, bleached, bony white birdcage, where his torso should be. Because he has no lungs, Henry Shade must trap small animals, lock them in his chest-cage, and use them to breathe for him.

In the pocket of his long blue coat, he keeps a damp, foul-smelling handkerchief, which gives off a nasty fume that tranquillizes his victims and keeps them from waking up. He then locks the sleeping animal in his chest-cage, and his gilled windpipe forces its way into the poor creature's mouth, like some infernal eel, leeching off of the air that it breathes.

The captive animals have to breathe twice as hard, and do not last very long. When they finally die of exhaustion, Henry puts them in his pot and boils them up for his supper.

No one has seen the old man in the village for nigh-on twenty years. The rise of such modern things as double-glazed windows, triple-locking security doors, and intruder alarm systems has forced Henry away from the town. These days he stays in the deep of the woods, chasing foxes and wild rabbits for the air in their lungs.

'. . . Which is why the lady in the Post Office won't talk to me any more,' finished Grandad, as irrelevantly as he had started. Unfortunately, by the time he had done with all his unnecessary footnotes and sub-plots, Iris had fallen fast asleep. She had heard almost all of his story – the important parts at least – but her eyes were tired and she could not keep even one of them open any longer. She lay curled up on her side, gently pushing at her loose front tooth as she sucked on her thumb.

It was a stuffy summer's night in the spare bedroom. When Grandad decided to leave the window open a crack, it unfortunately did not occur to him that he might let in more than just the cool air.

In the small grey hours, before dawn's first blush, the crooked old fingers of Henry Shade once more came a-scratching and a-rattling at the town's windows and doors.

Henry was sick; he was growing too weak and too slow to catch wild animals in the woods. He had not taken a breath of air for a month. He remembered the easy pickings he had found in the old days, and hoped that in his long absence the townsfolk had grown complacent enough to leave themselves unprotected again. His withered fingers tested every house he came to, looking for windows ajar, or doors unbolted. It was not long before his long, rangy arms found the open upstairs window of Iris's room. With a crooked grin, he gripped the window-ledge and heaved himself up.

A cloud of moths fluttered out of Henry's coat as he climbed in. He was so tall that, even hunched over, his white flaky head touched the ceiling. He paused for a moment to study the sleeping forms of the little girl and the cat. The room was silent, but for the seething beat of insect wings, and the soft rasp of his dry, breathless throat. He watched the gentle rise and fall of their bodies and dreamed of his very own set of lungs, fresh-filling with air.

His fingers twitched for the little girl, but . . . perhaps that was one step more than he was willing to take. It was one thing to steal sleeping animals, but taking sleeping children was too much. He was desperate enough to come back to the village after all these years, but he would not stoop to snatching little girls. The cat would suffice.

Henry pulled his flea-bitten handkerchief from his coat pocket and stroked it over Inky's sleeping face. The fumes from the cloth ensured that the cat did not wake as he scooped her limp little body up and shut her in his bleached and bony white chest-cage.

As he turned back towards the open window to leave, Iris – who had been lying awake for the last few minutes, watching Henry through one open eye – sat up in bed and called after him.

'Henry Shade!' she cried. 'Please don't take my grandad's cat away!'

Startled by the unexpected outburst, Henry Shade turned and looked at the little girl. Even if he could remember how to talk, he hadn't the breath to do so, so he simply blinked his shark-black eyes and cocked his head quizzically to one side.

'I bet a little cat like Inky doesn't last very long having to breathe for two, eh, Henry?' asked Iris, boldly.

Henry creased his brow in puzzlement and slowly shook his head no.

'I bet I could last much longer than Inky. I'm only small, but I have very strong, healthy lungs. I could last for days and days,' offered the little girl.

Henry leaned in close enough to feel Iris's healthy young breath on his face. Moths fluttered in her face. She could see the purple veins throbbing sluggishly in his temples.

'I'll make you a deal, Henry Shade,' said Iris, bravely staring straight back into his lifeless eyes. 'If you let Inky go, I'll take her place and breathe for you, for . . .' Iris quickly thought up a convincing length of time, '. . . four days. But you have to promise to let me go afterwards, and to never come back to this house again.'

The old man looked down at the little black cat lying unconscious in his chest-cage, and then looked Iris up and down. He bit on his crumbly bottom lip with his fractured teeth. The breath of a healthy little girl certainly was tempting. Perhaps if he really did let her go afterwards, it would be OK. . .

Iris held her breath for his decision, nervously working at her loose tooth with her tongue. Finally, Henry nodded his agreement.

The crooked old man placed the sleeping cat gently back on the bed, and held open the door to his bleached, bony white chest-cage. Crouching down, he beckoned the little girl inside with a gnarly finger. Iris climbed in and sat herself down in the bottom of the cage.

But clever Iris had a plan. Once out of Henry's view, she began tugging urgently at her loose front tooth with her fingers. As Henry's eely windpipe snaked down towards her, hungry for her young breath, she took one last wrench on her tooth and pulled it free from its gums. When the eager airway reached her lips she blew with all her might, spitting the pointy little tooth up into his throat.

Henry choked and gagged with shock as Iris's tooth

lodged in his windpipe. Normally, he might have survived such a blockage – he could go for several weeks without breathing, after all – but in his weakened and air-starved state, the surprise was just . . . too much to swallow.

The man-with-no-lungs' heart gave out, and frail old Henry Shade gurgled, spluttered and died. He toppled to the bedroom floor in a moth-ridden, blue-coated, spaghetti-haired old heap.

The next day, Iris Ventolin went with her grandad to the pet shop. She spent the rest of the afternoon catching up on her sleep in a big cosy armchair in the conservatory, with Inky the cat curled up snugly in her lap. Inky purred softly, and lay with one eye open to watch Grandad's new pet budgerigar chirp contentedly in its bleached, bony white cage.

Bottled Up

Stephanie Jackson

As the last letter was pressed down triumphantly on the keyboard, Ellie sat back with a look of smug satisfaction on her face. Everything that she had wanted to scream at Beth was down in print: it was off her chest and she hadn't even said a word! Obviously, she had no intention of sending the e-mail. Well, that's not strictly true, she definitely had the desire. Oh yes, she could see it now; Beth clicking the mouse to open her mail box, the red blotches of rage creeping up her throat and invading her face as her eyes scanned the screen, the spluttering noises that would emerge from her mouth as she grabbed her voice-activated mobile and screamed 'ELLIE!!!'

The bedroom door flung open. 'Ellie, can't you hear me shouting you from downstairs?' It was Ellie's mum, who by now had fully entered the room, completely ignoring the 'Do Not Disturb' sign on the *outside* of the door. Ellie slammed down on the return key, aiming to remove the writing from the screen, unaware that she had actually *sent* the e-mail! She spun around, smiling sweetly in an attempt to hide the guilty look on her face, and innocently replied, 'Sorry, Mum, didn't hear you. What can I do for you?'

Her mum frowned and paused in thought for a few seconds. When she spoke, she sounded quite cross. 'Well, Ellie, there are a few things that you can do for me. I've just been on the phone to Sue Smedly, Beth's mum.' Ellie's eyes opened a little wider and her heart began beating nervously fast. She wasn't sure of what to say, but that didn't matter, as her mum had no intention of stopping. 'Anyway, it seems that Beth has been unbearable this weekend. She's flitted between grumpiness, tears and tantrums, and her mum believes that *you* are responsible. Would you like to explain exactly what you have done this time, so that I can look Sue in the eye tomorrow morning?'

She was very serious, you could tell by the authoritative way she placed her hands on her hips. Ellie just lowered her head. Tears were stinging her eyes, but she was more angry than upset. It was so unfair and just *so* typical of Beth to turn it all around.

'It's not my fault, Mum. I never said anything to her! I know you've heard that before, but it's really true this time. Honestly, Mum, she's been really nasty lately and said some horrid things and. . .'

It was too late for excuses. Her mum put up her hand to indicate silence and then shook her head in disbelief. 'I'm really tired of this, Ellie. I've had enough to cope with, don't you think? I mean, what would your dad say to all this hassle?'

Ellie clenched her jaw. She hated it when her mum used her dad to make her feel guilty. Viciously, she spat back, 'Oh yeah, I'd like to know that myself!'

Her mum looked furious and a little puzzled, 'Just watch yourself lady, you can't speak to me like that. And what on earth do you mean? What do you want to know?'

Ellie was bright red with fury, but she knew that she wouldn't win this one. Through gritted teeth she replied, 'Nothing, it doesn't matter'.

They both took a second to draw a deep breath. Her mum came closer to her, touched her hand, and said more gently, 'Perhaps you should stay up here tonight and think carefully about the kind of person you want to be. You know darling, things will get easier, but bullying your friends won't help.' The door closed abruptly. Ellie was alone again, with only her thumping heart for company.

The next morning at school was predictably awful. Beth had received the e-mail, printed it out, and distributed it amongst the class. Miss Spencer got hold of a copy and rapidly scanned over it. Her face didn't give much away but she looked very disappointed as she folded it into her diary. 'Well, this is not the best start to the week, is it?' she said, glancing round the class. 'I'll have every other copy on my desk now please, and then you can all sit down and look at your Literacy books.

Beth and Ellie, I'd like to see you both at break, no arguments.'

Ellie was so embarrassed that she couldn't look at anyone. The tears were just a blink away from rolling down her face, and her head was spinning. Where would she sit? No one wanted her near them, and Abigail Richards had already hidden her pencil case. She knew it was childish of them, but it hurt all the same. Feeling seriously humiliated she took a pencil from the class-pot and sat alone on a table near the front.

By breaktime, Ellie was very frustrated. Miss Spencer had realised quite quickly what was going on amongst the girls in her class, and had given Ellie some individual work to keep her occupied. But this meant that the other girls had even more opportunity to push her out of the group. Her sense of injustice swelled up inside and she felt ready to burst.

When everyone was outside, Miss Spencer called the girls together. 'Now, who wants to explain why two of my best girls are falling out in such an awful way?' Both girls just sat quietly. 'OK then. Ellie, can you tell me what this is?' She put the e-mail on the desk in front of them.

Ellie inhaled deeply, 'I wrote that Miss, but sending it was a mistake. I just wanted to get things off my chest and I don't keep a diary, not since my dad. . .' she trailed off and put her head in her hands.

Beth looked up at her and felt a sharp twinge of guilt

about handing the e-mail out in class.

Miss Spencer's voice was soothing, 'It's OK, Ellie, I know why you don't keep a diary. I know that it still hurts you to think about your dad, but that doesn't explain why you have written these things to Beth.' She turned to Beth, 'Can *you* help to enlighten me, Beth?'

Ellie had begun to cry. Beth realised that she had hurt her friend by spreading the e-mail, just as much as she had been hurt by the e-mail itself. She knew that she shouldn't have said what she did, and had been wracked with guilt all weekend. 'Miss, it's my fault. I said some things on Friday that I shouldn't have said. I thought it was funny at the time, but I wasn't thinking about how Ellie felt. Everyone was laughing so I just carried on.'

Beth was looking very pale and worried, and Miss Spencer knew that she was telling the truth. 'What did you say on Friday that made Ellie so angry?'

Beth tried not to look at Ellie; she was the embarrassed one now. 'I said that her mum was going out with Gordon Townsend's dad. I heard it from someone in Year 4 and once I had told Abigail, it just sort of got out of control.' Her voice became squeaky, 'I'm really sorry, Ell. I wasn't thinking about how much it would upset you.'

Ellie looked across at her friend. Perhaps she really was sorry for what she said, but Ellie couldn't help believing that it might be true and that she had been the last to find out. She sighed. 'It's OK, I suppose. I'm sorry for calling you names in the e-mail, I was just so angry with you for saying that my mum was dating someone. I don't want it to be true; she can't have forgotten my dad so soon.' Her voice had gone shaky and Miss Spencer decided that she had had enough.

'Ellie, I'm sure that your mum hasn't forgotten your dad and that she will explain everything when she finds out why you two have been falling out. I'm going to let your mum know about this, so that she can understand why you have been so upset. But she will also find out about this e-mail, and I doubt she'll be too impressed. You had both better think about how best to explain this to your mums. OK, go out to break, there's still a few minutes left.' She gave them a warm smile and they both walked out into the sunny playground.

Later that day, Ellie's mum was waiting just outside the gate as usual. She told Ellie that Miss Spencer had rung her earlier to explain. 'I'm sorry for thinking that it was your fault that Beth had a bad weekend. Turns out that she was feeling guilty for saying what she did on Friday. Come on, I'm taking you for an ice cream so that we can talk.' Ellie linked arms with her mum and felt happier that they were friends again. But she still felt worried about her mum and Gordon's dad being a couple. She couldn't bear the thought of Gordon being her little brother, or of his dad becoming her *new* dad.

They walked along in silence, but Ellie's mum held her arm very closely to her and kept looking down and smiling knowingly. When they reached the park, Ellie chose her ice cream and they sat down.

'Darling, you know how much I love you, and that I always will, no matter what.'

Ellie felt embarrassed about the tears in her eyes, 'I know, Mum, I just feel like I'm always to blame when you're upset. I wish I could make you happy, then you wouldn't have to date Gordon's dad.'

Her mum's face creased into a large smile, 'I'm not going out with Gordon's dad, silly – he's definitely not my type!' They both began to laugh and her mum squeezed her tightly. 'I will always love your dad very, very much and I know that he would be as proud of you as I am. And, if the day comes when I think that I might be able to love someone else, someone as kind as your dad was, then I promise I will let you know straightaway. Your happiness will always come first, and your opinion is very important to me.'

Ellie leaned into her mum and felt the warmth of the late afternoon sun, as it shined down on them in the park. It may only be the two of them now, but she knew they were a family.

Gran and the Highwayman

PAOLA THOMAS

Felicity stared at the blank sheet of paper, chewed her little fingernail, and started to draw tiny lovehearts in the corner with her purple glitter pen. The throaty roar of a motorbike echoed down the close. Felicity pulled a face and shut her project folder. *Botheration*, she thought – and other words a ten-year-old girl really shouldn't be thinking – *Gran is the last thing I need.*

A few moments later, a voice sang through the letterbox, 'Coo-ee! It's only me,' followed by her mother's yell of 'Felicity, get that door will you? That'll be your gran. Just in time for tea, as usual.'

Felicity trudged down the stairs and opened the front door to an even weirder apparition than normal. She'd seen the biker's leather jacket and trousers before, of course, though not for the first time she wondered where Gran had managed to find them in a big enough size. No, it was the daffodils in Gran's hair – now rather squashed and bedraggled – which were unusual. Lulabella, Gran's Yorkshire Terrier, was similarly garlanded.

'I thought it would be nice to celebrate spring,' Gran said.

Felicity rolled her eyes.

Soon they were all sitting down to cottage pie. Gran had changed out of her leathers into a swirly-patterned kaftan, which looked like it had been made out of a pair of old curtains.

'Do you like my new kaftan?' Gran asked Felicity's mother. 'I had it made out of a pair of old curtains.'

Felicity's mother rolled her eyes.

They had reached a lull in the cottage pie when Gran turned to Felicity.

'So, my girl, why are you looking like a wet November weekend? You should be full of the joys of spring, tra-la!'

Felicity was glad they were sitting at the table, otherwise she was sure Gran would have done a little dance.

'Oh, it's this stupid project I'm doing for school. It's on Local History and I thought I'd do Black Jack the Highwayman, but four other people in my class are doing him as well, and I can't find out anything about him and it has to be in next week.' The words came tumbling out in a rush.

'But that sound most intriguing,' said Gran, 'why don't we see what we can do after tea?'

After an enormous helping of apple crumble, Gran folded up her napkin and dabbed at her fuchsia lips. 'Do you want to show me what you've done so far?'

Felicity didn't. The only thing she had in her project

folder was a rather good, so she thought, drawing of Nell, Black Jack's horse. Gran was less than impressed.

'Hmm. Is anyone using the computer?' she asked.

Felicity's older brother was out somewhere, so they settled themselves in front of the computer in his bedroom. Felicity wished that Gran's perfume wasn't quite so overpowering.

'But Gran, I've just been looking, there's nothing there.'

'Huh, you young people, you have no idea when it comes to the Internet.'

Soon, Barbie-pink nails were flying across the keyboard and reams of paper began whizzing off the printer.

'I think you'll find that helpful,' said Gran.

A mobile phone beeped. Gran rummaged in her handbag, pulled out her phone, held it at arm's length and peered at the screen.

'Oh goodness, I'm supposed to be playing whist with the vicar. Must dash,' she said.

It was Saturday morning and Felicity was reading through Gran's Internet discoveries.

Apparently, Black Jack had held up stage-coaches on the main road out of town in the 1730s and many pubs along that road had been named 'The Black Horse' in his honour. According to legend, he had been hiding in one of the houses in town when the magistrates had come to arrest him.

The telephone rang. The answerphone clicked in and a familiar voice rang round the house. 'Felicity, are you there? I've just been talking to my friend Bill at the library. He says he has something to show you.'

Twenty minutes later, the motorbike, this time with a sidecar attached, roared up the drive and came to a screeching halt. Felicity ran out of the front door, took a yapping Lulabella into her arms and jumped into the sidecar. It was a warm spring day and the interior smelt strongly of stale dog and hot leather. Felicity shut her eyes and held on tight as Gran wove at top speed through the Saturday morning traffic.

They came careering to a stop in the car park next to the library. Felicity emerged, dazed and blinking into the sunshine, feeling extremely queasy. Lulabella jumped out and Felicity just managed to grab her before she ran straight into the path of an enormous BMW. Lulabella clearly had the same attitude to traffic as her owner. Gran removed her sparkly purple helmet and patted her burgundy perm with a beringed hand. At least there were no daffodils today.

They walked into the library. Gran waved at a cheerful-looking man stamping books behind the counter. 'Coo-ee Bill!' she called. Everyone in the library made shushing noises. Felicity blushed. Bill came over to greet them.

'Ah, so you must be Felicity, your gran had told me all about you. I understand you're an expert on the life of Black Jack the highwayman.' Felicity felt herself blushing again and wished that Gran wasn't quite so prone to exaggeration.

They walked over to one of the shelves and Bill pulled out two large books, bound in rich red leather, of a slightly darker colour than Gran's hair. They were very, very beautiful and clearly very old.

'These are a history of the town written by a local farmer. They were published in 1862,' Bill said.

'Oh,' said Felicity, 'about a hundred and thirty years after Black Jack was captured.'

'Well, I see we really do have an expert on our hands,' said Bill, admiringly. 'I wanted to show you some pictures of what the town looked like in those days.'

Bill pulled on a pair of gloves and started to turn the pages. The shiny pages of illustrations were protected by crisp sheets of tissue paper.

'Here are some photographs taken just before the book was published. Look, here's the High Street.'

It was almost completely unrecognisable; no buses, no cars, no brightly-coloured shop fronts; trees and open fields where Sainsbury's now stood. But wait, there was the church, and that building there looked like 'The Rat and Carrot'. Felicity examined the sign outside the pub.

'Is that a black horse?'

Bill bent down to look at it more closely and Gran pulled out a pair of bright blue glasses decorated with diamanté butterflies.

'Well, it should be,' said Bill. 'That pub was called "The Black Horse" until a few years ago.'

'But pubs where Black Jack stayed were always called "The Black Horse"!' Felicity exclaimed.

Bill nodded even more admiringly. 'Gracious, I've always wondered where that name came from. Let's see if it's mentioned in here.' He traced through the index with a gloved finger, murmuring under his breath. The tissue crackled as he turned to another page.

'It says here that Black Jack would meet his cronies in this pub whenever he was in town and was reputed to have hidden in a nearby house for over a month before being captured by the magistrates.'

'I wonder which house it was,' said Gran. Bill turned to another page, which showed an engraving of the High Street in 1799 from a different direction. The church was still there, and the pub. The only other building visible was an old stone cottage, a bit further along from the pub.

'Perhaps that was the house,' said Bill.

'How very exciting!' said Gran.

'Shhh,' said a sour-faced woman at a nearby table.

'That's my friend Miss Peabody's house,' continued Gran loudly, ignoring the sour-faced woman completely. 'Perhaps it's haunted by Black Jack.' Gran raised her arms in the air and was just about to start making ghost noises when Bill stared at her.

'I'll try and wangle an invitation to tea,' she said to

Felicity in a loud whisper.

★

Felicity patted her project folder with pride. Now, as well as the rather nice drawing of Nell, it included an account of the Black Jack story, photocopies of the pictures of the High Street, a new photograph of the 'Rat and Carrot' taken by Felicity herself, plus an interview with 'a local man' (Library Bill) full of memories of the days when it had been called 'The Black Horse.' Surely it would one of the best projects in the class now?

Felicity put a new film into her camera. Gran and Lulabella were due to arrive any minute to take her to Miss Peabody's. While she waited, Felicity flicked through a rather dull book on local history that Bill had suggested she borrow. Suddenly, the words 'Black Jack' caught her eye.

'There is a strong local tradition that Jack Bradshaw, known as Black Jack, went into hiding at a local house before he was arrested by the magistrates. This house has never been identified and there is no evidence whatsoever to support the legend, which would appear to be nothing but hearsay and gossip.'

Felicity felt as if someone had given her a beautifully wrapped present and then snatched it away at the last moment. The book was right, of course. They hadn't uncovered any real evidence at all, just some local stories and the name of a pub.

The sound of a motorbike coming up the drive was followed by Gran's familiar 'Coo-ee!' through the letterbox. Felicity shut the book with a bang. She really wasn't in the mood for Miss Peabody's now.

Ten minutes later, Felicity emerged queasily from the sidecar with Lulabella in her arms. Miss Peabody, all snowy white hair and faded cardigan, was standing on the doorstep, looking exactly how an old lady ought to look.

She ushered them into her dainty sitting-room. 'Of course, it's all very different from how it would have been in Black Jack's time,' she said, handing round a plate of delicious-looking cream cakes. 'But I'm told the house dates from around 1670, so it was definitely standing in Black Jack's day.'

'I was reading something today that said it was all just a legend and that no one had ever found any evidence to back it up,' Felicity blurted out.

'Fiddlesticks,' said Gran. 'I don't believe those historians for one moment. I can feel it in my bones that Black Jack spent his last days in this very room.'

Felicity looked around and tried, without success, to imagine Black Jack sitting on the rose-covered sofas, sipping tea from the delicate china cups.

'Gertrude, my dear,' said Gran. 'Are there any ghosts here?'

At that very same moment, a huge crash came from the room next door, accompanied by the most bloodcurdling shriek. Miss Peabody screamed, Felicity yelped and Gran dropped her plate and three chocolate éclairs, which landed in a creamy, chocolaty heap on Miss Peabody's Persian rug. Lulabella started barking from another room.

'Come with me,' said Gran, leading the way out of the sitting-room. Miss Peabody and Felicity looked at each other, and followed several paces behind.

In the next room scenes of devastation awaited them. China figurines lay in smithereens on the floor. Lulabella was dancing and yapping in front of the huge old fireplace, while a spitting, angry tabby cat was jumping as high as it could up the chimney. Both were trying to catch a small sparrow, which was fluttering in terror round the fireplace.

'Ponsonby! Whatever are you doing?' shouted Miss Peabody, gathering the struggling cat in her arms.

Gran leapt to open the window and the tiny bird flew out as if pursued by the hounds of hell. 'Goodness gracious,' said Gran. 'That poor little bird must have fallen down the chimney.'

Felicity wasn't really listening. Instead, she and Miss Peabody were examining an object wrapped in sackcloth, which had fallen down the chimney and into the fireplace.

'This must have caused the crash,' said Felicity.

'Indeed,' said Miss Peabody. 'One of these ridiculous animals must have dislodged it with all that leaping about in the fireplace.'

The sackcloth was covered in a thick layer of dust, soot and grime. Gingerly, Felicity started to peel it away to reveal a very old wooden box. The two old ladies twittered like excited birds.

Felicity tried and failed to lift the lid of the box. 'I think it's locked!'

'Leave it to me,' said Gran. 'Gertrude, I shall require a knife, a hammer and a wire coathanger.'

A few moments later, Miss Peabody had returned with the necessary equipment. Gran flexed her fingers, poked at the lock with the hook on the coathanger, slid the knife round the edge of the box, and then bashed at the lock with the hammer. The box sprang open.

'Knitting,' said Gran, flexing her fingers again, 'is excellent for keeping the fingers supple.'

Felicity wiped her hands on her jeans and opened the box. Inside she could see gold. Gold coins. And lots of them. Felicity scooped them up and let them run between her fingers, like so many pebbles on a beach. Gran let out a long, low whistle. Lying under the coins were two antique guns, both with beautifully engraved brass trimmings. Felicity ran her fingers along their smooth, conker-coloured handles and picked up one of the coins. On one side was a picture of a curly-haired man with *Georgius II* written round the edge. 'I wouldn't want to meet him on a dark night,' remarked Gran.

The other side showed a coat of arms and the date *1733*.

'Oh, wow!' whooped Felicity. 'The dates are right! These could have been hidden by Black Jack!'

The following day, Felicity was standing outside Miss Peabody's cottage being photographed by the local paper. A small crowd had gathered, Library Bill had arrived, and somehow Felicity's class teacher had muscled in on the act.

'Oh, Felicity has always been one of my star pupils,' she was saying to the reporter from the *Echo*, though funnily enough she had never written anything of the sort in Felicity's school report.

'I understand your findings are going to be displayed at the local museum,' said the reporter, turning to Felicity, 'and that they have confirmed that the pistols and coins could well have belonged to Black Jack the Highwayman. You must be very proud.'

'Oh, I am,' said Felicity. 'But really, I couldn't have done anything without Library Bill, Miss Peabody, Ponsonby the cat, Lulabella and most especially my gran. Even if she is a bit of a pain.' And she went over to Gran, who was wearing a particularly striking hat with bright blue birds on it, and hugged her.

Georgina's Run

Caroline Otterson

A groan echoed around the changing room. Twenty-five girls had just finished getting out of their unattractive school uniforms (navy blue blazer and skirt, turquoise shirt and – wait for it – red socks!) and into their P.E. kits of red T-shirt and navy shorts. The twenty-sixth girl, Georgina Jones, was a bit slow. 'Get on with it, Jones,' hissed Miss Heffer, angrily. Miss Heffer telling her off was nothing new. She didn't know what she had done, but the P.E. teacher always told her off more than anyone else in the class. She never let anything go, and she always called her 'Jones', even though she called all the other girls by their first names. Generally, Georgina was pretty well-behaved and got on well with her teachers: the only other one who seemed to dislike her was Mr Rogers, who taught them geography.

It was the first day of the summer term, and nobody wanted to do what Miss Heffer had just announced – with more than hint of a smile – go on a cross-country run. They hadn't been expecting this, as they usually only had to slog around the cross- country course in winter. *Three miles around muddy fields and woods: great!* thought Georgina.

Miss Heffer put on a leather jacket and motorcycle helmet. As usual, she would ride around the course with the girls, in case any of them decided to take it easy. It was strange though, that despite the fact that Miss Heffer always started out with them, and was on her motorbike, she only just got back to the school before they did. She seemed to just disappear at some point on the course. There were a number of different rumours in class gossip. Becky Andrews said she was stopping for a secret smoke. Paula Watkins said that she was having secret meetings with Mr Rogers: she had seen them smiling at each other in the corridor, so there must be something going on. Georgina was curious about the woman who made her P.E. lessons such a misery, but told herself that there was no time to think about it now. She had to get the knots out of the laces in her trainers and start running as soon as possible, otherwise Miss Heffer would really shout at her. She had seemed particularly tetchy this morning, so Georgina would have to watch her step even more than usual.

By the time she had sorted out her footwear and got started, the other girls had gone, and Miss Heffer had revved up her bike and set out after them, riding uncomfortably close behind poor little Lauren Thomas and the other stragglers. For once, she seemed to have forgotten about Georgina. Relieved, Georgina set off as fast as she could, across the playground, round the back of the assembly hall and towards the field, where the boys were getting stuck into a game of football. A few of them called and teased her as she puffed past them, trying to keep Miss Heffer and the girls in sight.

As they left the school grounds, the course went up a steep hill before turning into some scruffy woodland. Georgina always found this bit difficult, but today she made a real effort to go as fast as she could, to try and catch up with the others. When she got to the top of the hill though, they were all out of sight. At this point on the course, there was a fork in the road, and two possible routes that runners could be told to follow. Up to now, they had always taken the right-hand route, which was a bit shorter, but Georgina saw Miss Heffer's motorbike tracks taking the left-hand route, going into the trees rather than past them. Groaning at the thought of running an extra half mile, she turned left and set off after the class.

After about two minutes of hard running, Georgina came across a motorbike leaning against a tree. It was definitely Miss Heffer's bike: Georgina had stared at its number plate enough times to be sure that she would always remember it. This was interesting. Maybe she would be the one to solve the mystery of what it was that the P.E. teacher got up to during these cross-country runs. She laughed at the idea of herself as a schoolgirl sleuth and looked at her surroundings.

Behind the motorbike were a few scrubby trees. Beyond them was an old wooden hut, in a bad state and covered in graffiti. Perhaps this was where Miss Heffer went. Very quietly, Georgina approached the hut, ready to run at world-record pace if the teacher should appear. She heard two voices whisper. *So*, she thought, *Becky wins: Heffer is meeting somebody here after all.* Then, she saw a wisp of smoke coming from the cracked window. *And Paula was right too: she is having a crafty smoke.* Georgina wanted to make sure it was Miss Heffer, and to find out who the other person was, so she had to get closer. She took a deep breath, then crept up to the hut. The smoke and whispers continued. There was no sign that anyone had heard her. She found a convenient hole in the wooden wall of the hut and, taking another deep breath, put her face up to it and peered inside.

It took a moment for her eyes to get accustomed to the dark, and then another for her mind to make sense of what she was looking at. *Two . . . dragons!* There were two dragons, one red, one green, breathing fire and whispering. Commonsense and everything she had ever read told Georgina that she must be mistaken: these were mythical beasts. Mythical – not real! If anyone ever saw such things, it would be some clever posh boy at boarding school or someone visiting a rambling stately home, not an ordinary girl like her in the scruffy woods between her school and the tower blocks.

She looked again. Now she was sure. Bizarre as it

seemed, there really were two huge scaly lizards there, breathing fire and everything. Even stranger was the fact that one of them was wearing Miss Heffer's leather jacket and carrying her helmet, while the other had Mr Rogers' trademark spotted bow-tie round his neck. *Have they eaten Miss Heffer and Mr Rogers?* wondered Georgina at first, but once she listened to their whispering voices, she knew that wasn't it. She had no idea how it could be, but it was clear that these two beasts actually *were* the two teachers from her school.

Her astonishment drove away all thoughts of being quiet and not being discovered. 'I must be going mad!' she said out loud. Immediately, the dragons stopped their whispered conversation. They came out of the door very quickly, looking to see who had spoken. Georgina was terrified. If Miss Heffer shouted and snapped at her normally, what would she do to her as a dragon?

'Who is there?' demanded Heffer-dragon.

'Come out!' said Rogers-dragon.

Georgina looked around for somewhere to hide. The trees might have been a possibility if they had been a bit taller or bushier but, as it was, they were useless. She moved behind one of the walls of the hut, but realised that it would only be a short time before they saw her there. The only thing for it was to do what she was supposed to be doing in the first place, and run.

Just as Georgina took her first few steps towards the track, Heffer-dragon's voice repeated her question,

'Who is there?'

Not thinking straight, and used to doing what she was told by teachers, Georgina turned and answered 'Georgina Jones, Miss', then promptly tripped over a tree root and fell on to the muddy ground. She cowered there for a second, expecting the worst, and not really wanting to look as the fire-breathing reptile/P.E. teacher toasted her. For a few seconds, nothing happened. She waited a little longer. Still, nothing happened. 'Oh, just get it over with!' said Georgina, turning her head around to face the beast.

The beast, however, was not toying with her, waiting to strike. Instead, the green dragon was running back towards the red one beside the hut. Soon, both were whimpering in a pathetic fashion, their fires put out by abundant dragon-tears. 'Don't hurt us, G-g-g-eorgina!' they cried.

This was really strange. Georgina wondered if it was a trap. Were they trying to lure her in so that they could incinerate her secretly in the hut? They looked genuine though and, when she took a small step towards them, they flinched and moved back. The dragons were scared of her!

She felt a little sorry for them now, but most of all, she felt very very curious. She approached them. They retreated until their backs were against the wall of the hut. 'I'm not going to hurt you,' she said.

There was an awkward silence. Georgina was not sure how to begin to ask what was going on. 'So, you're dragons,' she commented, at the risk of being blunt. The dragons nodded. 'Erm, how do you manage to look like people then? Is there some sort of spell for that?' she asked. The dragons nodded twice more. 'But I don't get it,' she said, scratching her head, 'why don't you look like people now, and why are you scared of me when you are great big, fire-breathing monsters and I'm just a thirteen-year-old girl?'

'I object to being called a monster,' said Heffer-dragon. 'There's no need to be offensive: we are *beasts*, noble beasts of an ancient race, and there aren't many of us left any more.'

'You are right to observe that we have powerful disguising and fire-emitting capabilities,' said Rogers-dragon. 'We can pass as human and we can barbecue anyone and anything that gets in our way most of the time, but we also have our limitations, and today is the one day of the year when we feel particularly vulnerable.'

'Why?' asked Georgina, 'what's so special about today. It's just the first day of term.'

She thought a bit more and said, 'April 23rd – St George's Day? Is that what you mean?'

The two dragons shuddered and nodded. 'I don't know why humans have to celebrate that man after what he did,' hissed Heffer-dragon, 'the dragon he slayed was a close personal friend, and the stories about her eating thousands of people were greatly exaggerated. She might have nibbled the odd princess when she was feeling peckish, but where's the harm in that? Whenever anyone mentions that thug "Saint" George in front of a dragon, it makes him so angry he can barely control himself. And on "St George's Day" as you insist on calling it, we simply can't keep ourselves under control. The disguise spell isn't strong enough to keep our dragon nature hidden, and our human appearance keeps fading away.'

'So – hang on,' said Georgina, 'the reason you don't like me is because of my name? Because it's Georgina, the feminine form of George?'

'Yes,' replied Heffer-dragon, 'to this day, we dragons are petrified of that name. We never say it, we hate to hear it, and we are terrified of anyone called George or Georgina. We can't stop ourselves thinking about that terrible man and what he did to poor, poor Agnes.'

At that moment, there was a quiet beeping sound: the school end-of-lesson bell. Georgina's mind was torn away from the frankly astonishing conversation she was having with the two dragons. It was, she realised, the end of the first period. The others would have been back in the changing room for ages, and wondering where she and the P.E. teacher were. No doubt all sorts of wild theories would be created. Miss Heffer obviously realised that she had to get back, too.

Georgina watched, amazed, as, with a big effort and a little chanting, she transformed herself back into a more or less human shape (though, now that she knew the truth, she did detect a greenish tinge to the teacher's face, and a slight scaliness on the hands).

Miss Heffer looked at her warily. 'Well, Jones,' she said, 'I think we will have to declare a truce. What you know about me and Mr Rogers could finish our careers. People are so prejudiced about dragons, and seem very reluctant to let them work with children. We are just lucky that nobody would ever believe you if you told them the truth.'

Georgina realised that she was right, and also saw that, as luck would have it, she had nothing to fear from the dragons. She had always rather disliked her name and, if her middle name hadn't been Doris, she might have insisted on using that. As it was, she saw that there were definite advantages to being called Georgina. She accepted a ride back to school on Miss Heffer's motorbike, and they made it back before the end of break.

In the next lesson, her friends asked her what had happened. Georgina gave them a vague story about falling over and hurting her ankle. 'We were scared that Heffer had done you in this time,' said Becky, 'she's always had it in for you, and she's such a *dragon*.' Georgina just smiled. She had a feeling that she was not going to have such a hard time in P.E., or geography, after this.

The Man Who Did Not Dream

Matthew Skelton

Once upon a time, there was a man who did not dream. Each night, he would put on soft pyjamas, tuck himself in bed, and prepare for a good night's sleep. Sometimes, he would wrinkle his nose once or twice, as if his feather pillow tickled him, or would stretch his toes until they touched the cool shallows at the foot of his bed, but most often he would just close his eyes and fall quickly, deeply, instantaneously asleep.

But he never dreamed.

Other people, when they heard about his condition, naturally felt very sorry for him and remarked that it must be very boring indeed to spend eight hours each night without a glimmer, or even a flicker, of a dream in his head. For they imagined that he must lie awake at night in his moon-coloured sheets, twiddling his thumbs and waiting for the sun to come up the following morning. But the little man simply smiled when he heard this and said that he had never passed a sleepless night in his life. He just lay in his bed and snugly slept. He was perfectly happy.

Nevertheless, he liked to hear other people discussing

their dreams, and listened closely while they described the giant giraffes, clockwork bees, or moving statues that ambled, buzzed or creaked across their minds at night. But sometimes they had what they called *nightmares*, which made him want to cover his ears like timid mice. He was too afraid to listen. He imagined fiery horses snorting steam in their dreams and heard hard heavy hoofs pounding and resounding in their skulls. He preferred funny dreams and would laugh at their oddity or invention.

He often wondered what it would feel like to dream. Perhaps, he thought, it was like wearing a wild, wonderful, woolly hat made from some magical material, with shimmering designs woven into it, that gradually came unravelled inside your head at night. Perhaps that's why some people woke up with electric hairdos, he thought, and spent so long brushing their hair each morning.

Or perhaps, dreaming was like fishing. Perhaps images darted back and forth all night long, as in an aquarium or a dark blue sea, until the morning light hooked or speared an image and it became a dream. Perhaps that was why most people remembered their dreams for only a short time after they woke up, since dreams were like slippery fishes, hard to hold on to.

But how could you sleep, he wondered, when so many strange images were swimming around in your head, never letting you rest? It made him sleepy just to think about it. Luckily, he never had to worry about such things for long, since all he had to do was close his eyes and he would fall quickly, deeply, instantaneously asleep.

But he never dreamed.

One morning, he woke up extra early and determined that this would be the day he found out what dreams were really like. He decided to see Mr Quiltpin, who owned a fashionable boutique in the High Street, for advice. If dreams were an invisible, extravagant hat that one could buy, then Mr Quiltpin would surely stock one in his size – or at least could order one for him – he thought.

A little bell tinkled above the shop door when he entered.

'I'll be right there,' called Mr Quiltpin from a back room.

The little man did not mind waiting. The boutique was full of garments that swirled and swayed on their hangers like dancers. Dresses curtseyed and waistcoats bowed. Shelves were stacked with lace, buttons, scarves, wigs, hats, gloves and bottles of perfume. It was like being invited to a fabulous ball.

Mr Quiltpin entered, sliding with short slippered footsteps across the marble floor. A large powdered wig sat like a swan on his head. He had put it on backwards in his haste.

'I have just had the oddest dream,' he said by way of introduction. 'I dreamt that I had misplaced my face and didn't know where to find it again.'

The little man remarked that this was certainly an odd dream to have and asked politely whether Mr Quiltpin had been able to locate his face again before he woke up.

'Oh yes, yes, most fortunately yes,' said Mr Quiltpin, readjusting his wig. His body was a long gesticulating curlicue in red fabric. His fingers were swollen with rings. 'In fact, I found my face just where I had left it,' he continued. 'In the mirror. But for the longest time I stumbled around looking for it. It was dreadful! Imagine having no eyes to see where you are going, no nose to sniff around corners, no ears to listen for the slightest sound, and no mouth to kiss your face when it returns!'

That did indeed sound horrible and the little man shuddered. He wondered if this was how the mannequins in the shop window felt.

'Oh, you have no idea,' said Mr Quiltpin, interrupting his thoughts. 'I rummaged in my suitcases, delved in my drawers, and even searched my pill-boxes looking for it, but I couldn't find my face anywhere. Without my eyes to guide them, my legs were like clumsy scissors and I tripped over them.'

Mr Quiltpin patted his face as if to remind himself that it was still there. To make doubly sure, he checked his reflection in each of several mirrors behind the counter.

Perhaps, if Mr Quiltpin experienced such terrifying

dreams, the little man thought, he might not be the best person to sell him a dream hat. Perhaps, he ought to try fishing for dreams instead. His eyes alighted on a spool of dark durable thread behind the counter and a sharp silver clasp. He had an idea.

'I would like several yards of your strongest thread,' the little man said, 'and this clasp.' Mr Quiltpin promptly wrapped the items in a paper parcel and the little man left the boutique with a package in his hand.

He hurried towards the sea.

The cobblestones in the road shone like brown and golden seashells in the warm sunlight and a cool breeze, touched with salt, skipped up the street to tickle his nose. Beyond, the water loomed like a huge whale.

At last, the little man reached the promenade and sat down next to several rugged fishermen on the pier. Between them, they held a variety of nets and fishing rods. Each studied the surface of the water intently, lost in thought. They were concentrating so deeply, in fact, they seemed asleep.

Then one of the fishermen looked up.

'Hello,' said the little man, unwrapping his thread and silver clasp from its package. With great care, he knotted the thread around the clasp, so that the knot resembled a small shimmering butterfly, and then tied the other end to his finger. Finally, he tossed his fancy handmade hook in the water. It disappeared quickly, as though a whale had gulped it.

'And what precisely are you hoping to catch with such a delicate little hook as that?' asked the fisherman nearest him, who had been watching him closely.

'I am going to catch a dream fish,' said the little man.

The other fishermen heard this and laughed. Even the seagulls joined in, looping overhead, shrieking.

'Well, then best of luck to you,' said the friendly fisherman with a nod and then went back to studying the surface of the sea, as though he could divine its thoughts.

The little man tried to do the same. It was fascinating. In each wave were different colours that swirled into each other and then swept apart. Black washed into indigo, which dissolved into blue, which deepened into purple, and then turned back into black. It was lovely to watch the colours blend and swirl; yet soon the little man felt his concentration slacken.

The mesmerising movement of the water made a gentle sucking noise as it lapped against the pier. It was like listening to a sleeper breathe and the sound made him want to take off his shoes and socks so that he could dangle his toes, like pebbles, in the water. He imagined sliding into the cool water, just as each night he climbed into the cool sheets of his bed. He was suddenly overwhelmed by a desire to yawn.

He looked at the other fisherman, all of whom seemed asleep. He blinked once, twice, but when he blinked for the third time, his eyes closed more heavily.

In his mind, he followed the length of thread down into the dark blue sea, where he could just imagine the end swaying back and forth like an empty strand of net. The silver clasp glinted. But then he felt something nibbling at the end of his thread. . . Softly, gently, it tugged at the line, like a thought at the back of his mind that he couldn't quite reach or an itch he couldn't quite scratch. Something was biting his hook!

He was immediately awake again and tried to reel it in, pulling with all his might on the line, battling with a curving, thrashing fish deep in the depths of the sea. He was amazed by how powerful the fish was. It seemed to pull him back and forth in loops and spirals, deeper and deeper into the sea, further into darkness. In fact, it was easier not to fight the fish at all, he found, but to give in to its pulling, sweeping movement and then yank back suddenly on the thread. He gave in a little and then pulled back. In this way, he gradually managed to coax the fish closer to the surface, just discerning its sleek outline in the water – its flash of silver, its thrust of gold.

At last, the fish emerged. It tossed the water off its body like a glossy coat. It was a beautiful fish. A dream catch.

It was, in fact, the king of fishes!

For the little man saw now that it was not simply covered in normal scales like other fishes, but was wearing a robe that glittered with the light of a thousand sequins. He was fascinated by the way the robe kept changing colour: silver, gold, ruby and bronze all flickered over its surface like an oil-slick on water. The fish also carried a little trident made from three sharp hooks, set in a piece of driftwood, in its left fin.

'I am the king of the fishes,' it said imperiously (with a slight lisp, because the clasp bit into its lip). 'I have existed since this sea was just a puddle and before you were born. I ask that you now let me go back to rule the other creatures in the dark blue sea. In return for my freedom, I will grant you one wish.'

The little man bowed. Most fairytales, he knew, offered their heroes and heroines as many as three wishes, but he would be happy with just one wish, so long as it came true. He explained that he had not been fishing for riches, or even for a member of royalty, but had simply hoped to catch a dream fish. He wished above all things to know what it felt like to dream.

'But I think you have learned that already,' said the fish. And then, before the little man could comprehend what the fish meant, it had detached the silver clasp from its lip and disappeared like a stream of water back into the sea. The little man watched while the broken seam of water stitched itself shut again. A broken piece of thread dangled from his finger.

After a while, he became aware of the other fishermen looking at him on the pier. 'So you've had no luck, then?' said the fisherman nearest him, pointing to the man's empty hands and his broken thread.

'Yes – er, no,' said the little man. He was not quite sure. He was about to hold out his hands in the air, measuring the size of the fish he had just caught, but then he shrugged and said, 'It was a dream fish, but it got away.'

Without another word, he packed up his things and went home.

★

And there, if you could have tiptoed after him, you would have seen him close his eyes later that night like little moons and would have seen freckles shine on his cheeks like stars. And if you could have listened to the darkness, you would have heard him snore, each breath popping and sizzling like a silver firework. And if you could have looked into his mind, you would have seen wave upon wave of beautiful colours dashing and darting there, broken every now and then by the flicker of an elusive fish-tail.

But he would have told you that he was not dreaming.

The Project

Hilary Ohene-Yeboah

Another project! Kirsty hated projects. What was the point of them? You just took information from one place and put it in another, without necessarily passing it through your brain. Oh well, it had to be done so she might as well start now.

School was a part of life that Kirsty put up with. She liked having a laugh with her friends, but lessons were generally a bore. She was clever, she knew that, but with the minimum of effort she managed to do all right. She'd learnt years ago, in primary school, that she could get a 'B' grade with very little work, so what was the point of slogging your guts out for an 'A'?

She turned on the computer and opened a new file. The title – she'd worry about the font later – 'Richard the Lionheart', or should it be 'Richard I' – it didn't really matter, did it? These history cards her mum had given her were quite good, with each card having a different aspect of the king's life. She'd got a couple of books from the library, too – so even if she didn't use them they'd look good in the bibliography. She began to type:

Introduction

This following project is about Richard the Lionheart, the king of England. He spent his whole life fighting in the Crusades against the Muslim Turks and only actually spent a year in England. I will tell you about him and his struggle against the Muslim Turks.

'Kirsty – food!' she heard her mum calling her from downstairs. Typical, just when she'd got started. Kirsty put the cursor on 'File' and then 'Save as'. She typed in 'Richard I', and ran downstairs for dinner. Her brother was already there at the table.

'I'm going on the computer after,' he said.

'No way, I'm doing school work,' Kirsty said. 'Mum, tell him'.

Dinner was over, and Kirsty sat down at the computer again. She opened the 'Richard I' file and looked puzzled. *I didn't use that font* she thought to herself. She read what she had written.

Just as she had written it. She scrolled down the page. What? She hadn't done this much. The words just went on and on. Then came a gap, half a page of nothing. Then it started again: Chapter 1. She scrolled on in disbelief, chapter 2, chapter 3, chapter 4 and on and on to chapter 11! What was in front of her was a complete project on Richard I, divided into chapters, spell-checked, headings underlined – all done! It was impossible, she'd only spent about ten minutes on it.

She left the last page on the screen and ran downstairs. 'Finished already?' asked Ian.

'Ian, Ian,' Kirsty ignored his question, 'Ian, did you do a project on Richard I for history in Year 7?'

'No, was that when you had to do anything from 1066 to 1700? I did Shakespeare and copied most of it from the one I'd done in primary school. Why?'

'It doesn't matter'.

Kirsty went back upstairs and looked at the screen again. She was half expecting to see just the first short paragraph that she had written before dinner. But no, it was just as she had left it, the last page of chapter 11. There was no explanation, but she wasn't going to switch off the computer and risk losing the project. Whatever was going on, she had a finished project in front of her and she wasn't going to waste it. She clicked on 'File' and 'Print' and within seconds she had a project on Richard I, all ready to put in a folder and hand in.

The next day started as usual; Kirsty woke up, got dressed and grabbed a half- buttered piece of toast before she started to run to school. On her way, Kirsty couldn't stop thinking about how her project just 'wrote itself'. Somehow, she was actually early for school that day.

She saw Laura and Hazel in the playground.

'Hi, guys,' Kirsty said as she walked towards them.

'Hi, Kirsty,' they said together.

'So, anything good happen over the weekend?'

'No, not really,' replied Laura.

'Have you two been working on your history projects?'

'Yeah, it took me ages just to do the first chapter,' groaned Hazel.

'It only took me ten minutes to do the whole project,' Kirsty said boastfully to herself.

'What?'

'Oh, nothing,' Kirsty quickly replied. The bell rang and the three started to walk to registration.

Later that week it was geography. They were doing earthquakes, which Kirsty actually found quite interesting. She was fascinated by the idea that children in Japan did earthquake-drill in the same way as children in Britain did fire-drill. They learnt about the big Kobe earthquake; Kirsty could vaguely remember hearing about it on the news. For homework, they had to write a newspaper article about the Kobe earthquake, using the facts that they had learnt, but making up eye-witness accounts. No problem, thought Kirsty.

Kirsty sat down at the computer that night. She clicked on 'Format' and chose three columns, might as well make it look something like a newspaper. Headline – 'Kobe Shakes', yes, that would do. Now where was that geography book? She'd better look up one or two facts, how far was Kobe from Tokyo? Kirsty walked across the room and reached down to get her exercise book out of her school bag. She took it back to the computer and gasped as she looked at the screen. There, in three columns, under the headline 'Kobe Shakes' was a whole page of print. She read it, yes the facts were all there just as she would have written them. It had happened again! Somehow, her homework was done! Kirsty printed off the single sheet and put it in a folder, then in her school bag. She couldn't go downstairs yet, they wouldn't believe she'd finished her homework already. She clicked on the games and began to play Spider Solitaire. Her mind was in a whirl. This was not possible. She went back over to her bag and took the folder out. It *was* true, there was the evidence – the article was there.

Kirsty was still in a daze the next day at school. Laura and Hazel raised their eyebrows towards each other behind Kirsty's back – she was acting rather strangely. They handed in their geography homework first lesson. Kirsty half expected to see a page of blank paper when she took hers out of the folder, but no, it was a neatly presented newspaper article. After break, it was history and they had their projects back. 'A plus' – Kirsty read her teacher's comments. She'd never read anything so flattering. 'Now you've shown what you can really do, Kirsty,' her teacher's voice broke into her thoughts, 'I knew you'd got it in you if you bothered to try.'

Kirsty was finding it difficult to think of anything except the strange homework assignments, but she still had other work to do. That night, she had some maths and she sat down to do it as soon as she got home. She wrote the title in her exercise book, 'Equations', and worked solidly for almost an hour. She wrote neatly and accurately and was confident that she had got them all right.

There was one other thing that she had to do that night. They didn't often have homework for PSE (Personal and Social Education). Most people didn't take the subject very seriously, and the pupils had a feeling that the teachers didn't either. The whole school did it once a week at the same time, with their form tutor. Kirsty's form tutor made it reasonably interesting, getting the class to chat about issues. She wasn't too worried if they didn't write anything, or if they only did a fraction of what was in her lesson notes, as long as they thought about things and expressed their opinions. This week, however, they'd been told to write a story; there was some sort of competition and they needed a few entries from each class. They'd been doing work about bullying and that's what the story had to be about. A few weeks ago, Kirsty wouldn't have bothered much about such work, but for some reason she decided to give it her best. She went to the computer and wrote the title 'The Bully'. Then she thought – what now? She hadn't a clue where to start. She nibbled at a nail on her little finger. Starting a story was always the hardest bit. Then she looked at the screen. Faster than she could read, words were appearing on the screen. One page, two pages, three pages, finished. Kirsty scrolled back to the top and read. It was brilliant, just what she'd have written, but better! She printed it off, put it in her bag and went downstairs.

The next day, Kirsty handed in her story to her form tutor who looked surprised and pleased. Laura and Hazel were surprised, too.

'I was thinking of doing it,' said Hazel, 'but I haven't started yet, it doesn't have to be in until next week.'

Later, it was English. For the past couple of weeks they'd been working on autobiographical writing. They'd had to write paragraphs about particular memories. Then Mr Lee set them their final task.

'I want you to imagine that you are someone who was born over a hundred years ago and write their autobiography. Try to think about the sort of life they would have led.'

Kirsty walked home slowly, thinking to herself about the autobiography she had to write. Would it happen again? Could she start with a line or two and then come back to find the story written? The whole thing was beginning to frighten her. It was impossible – things like this just didn't happen, not in real life, not outside stories or television. She thought about the project, the newspaper article, the story, all written for her. Her brother had used the computer and he hadn't said anything strange had happened. Kirsty shook her head, trying to shake the questions out of her mind.

'Hi, Mum, I'm home!' she called as she let herself in.

She heard a 'Hello' from the kitchen. 'How was your day?' asked her mother as she came through to the hall, wiping her hands on a towel. Then, without waiting for an answer, 'Don't just drop your things there.'

Kirsty picked up her school bag and carried it upstairs to her room. She went into the spare room and reached out to the computer. She hesitated, *No*, she thought to herself, *I'll leave it 'til later.* She went downstairs and turned on the television. 'Have you got any homework?' her mother asked.

'Yes, I'll do it later.'

'Well, don't leave it too late.'

Soon, it was later and Kirsty couldn't put it off any longer. She turned on the computer. What was this? Instead of the normal startup screen, the computer had gone straight to a document. The title: 'My Autobiography'. Kirsty stared open- mouthed, she hadn't even typed a single word and yet here was her assignment, complete. She began to read.

My name is Sarah Wallace and I was born in Haltwhistle on February 15th, 1890. I don't remember much of the first six years of my life except that I used to see my mother working from the time I got up until I went to bed. She was in the kitchen most of the time, making meals for my father and my two older brothers: breakfast first and while they were eating that she prepared their bait and put it in tins to take down the mine. When they had gone it was time for her to get my other two brothers ready for school. Then it was housework for the rest of the day. Washing took all day on a Monday, with a big kettle on the fire, constantly boiling, being emptied and boiling again. She filled the big copper in the scullery over and over again and rubbed and thumped the clothes, lathered them with a lump of soap and then rinsed them clean. Next, they went through the mangle, it was hard work turning that big handle.

One day was baking day, bread and cake and dumplings all cooked in the big coal-fired stove in the kitchen fireplace. There always seemed to be something to scrub, or wash, or rub, my mother never stopped.

When my father and the two oldest boys came home from the mine there was a big bath in front of the fire full of hot water and one by one, father first, they sat in it and scrubbed the black dust from their bodies. Even at five years old I was expected to run back and forwards with buckets of hot water.

Then at six years old, things changed – I went to school. My little world seemed to explode, there was so much I wanted to know. I read every book I could get, I asked questions of anyone who would answer. I looked at the big map of the world on the classroom wall and imagined sailing across the sea to Africa, or India or China. My hand was always the first to go up when the teacher asked a question. Learning was my life, my escape from reality. I never really allowed myself to believe that any of my dreams would come true, but the dreams were still there, deep down inside. There was more to life than what I had, what my mother had – and education had to be the key.

Four years of school, that is all I had, and now the dreams are over. It is the beginning of a new century and everyone is excited about what it will bring. The old queen cannot last long, but she will outlive me. I am ill, very ill, and I lie in bed, not even strong enough to read the book I so wanted to finish. I am only ten years old, but I have seen others waste away and I know that it will come to me.

There was no more. Kirsty felt a tear in her eye. 'Thank you,' she whispered, 'thank you.'

Hunters

Jayi Powell

Fana nodded his head. *Those animals are elephants.* The small leafy bush, from which he spied on the great creatures, hid him well. The early morning breeze which cooled his face, brought to him sweet scents of crushed leaves and stripped bark, as the elephants browsed in the glade.

Fana had never seen an elephant before. They were mere imaginings, conjured by the dance of the hunters in the flickering, uncertain light of their campfires. Fana's father always danced the dance of the elephant. He would bow at the waist, one arm trailing forward, sometimes curving slowly upwards, to wave his hand gently in the air. He held his other arm elbow high, pointing at the hunting stars, his hand pulled up his ribcage, almost to his armpit.

'It is the great ear of the elephant,' explained Fana's mother.

'Yes,' Grandfather always said, 'your father is the elephant. The elephant is your father.' Then he would nod gently as if his head was set on a spring, and clap his hands lightly together, raising a puff of dust which made them both sneeze.

Fana's father danced. He stripped imaginary trees of leaves, branch by branch, then tore strips of bark from their trunks. He lowered his head and uprooted trees, causing their roots to point skywards. He charged lions and human hunters alike, tossing them into the air, stamping them into the red earth, crushing them, kneeling on their bodies, goring them with his tusks.

Grandfather told Fana, 'One day, when you are a hunter, you will see the great elephants. And you will know them.'

Fana was in no hurry to see elephants, nor to become a hunter. Life was fine for a boy, with few responsibilities and many privileges.

The women-folk fawned on him, the ancients indulged him. He was first to be fed, last to be deprived. It was wonderful being a boy-child.

Even so, life was hard in the arid, semi-desert region where Fana's family wandered in their search for food. Often, the hunters would be unsuccessful and the women would not always find edible roots and berries. Only after the scarce falls of rain could soft shoots and leaves be added to the cooking pot.

Often, the hunters would be away for up to four days, travelling fast and far, searching for game. Sometimes, they would return to the camp with a few jackrabbits, or a small antelope. From time to time they would send for the family to move camp to where they had killed a large animal, perhaps the giant oryx, the desert *gemsbok*. They would cry for the death of the life it gave. They would dance its dance.

The family would feast for days on such a big animal. They would cook and eat until their hungry, flat stomachs stretched into bellies, round, smooth and overfull.

'You look like the moon,' Fana's grandfather would say, 'you are a melon.'

The day came when the hunters did not return from the hunt. And Fana's world changed. Four days passed, five, eight, ten. The young women stopped singing. Fights broke out.

Fana's grandfather berated them. 'You are sisters here. Be sisterly.'

They scowled and went to look for food. But soon, they began to sing softly together. Fana played in the shade of the hide shelter. Grandfather drew his *kaross* closer around his frail body and shivered.

'Why do they fight?' Fana asked his grandfather.

'They are hungry, and they are afraid.'

'Why are they afraid?' asked Fana. He drew lines in the dust with a twig.

Grandfather closed his eyes to shut out the question, but Fana persisted. 'Why, Grandfather?'

The old man sighed. 'It is their children,' he said, 'they need milk for the babies, and meat. They need the men to come back. They are afraid.'

'Are you afraid, Grandfather?' asked Fana.

'I am old. I am a man. Fear does not speak to me.'

He closed his eyes and slept.

Fana was hungry – his stomach called out for food like a chick in a bird's nest – but he was not afraid.

The hunters had been away for fourteen days and the camp was almost silent. The women collected firewood, swept the shelters, did all the normal chores. However, they all spoke in low tones, there was no singing, no joking, none of the usual banter. Even their arguments, jealousies and spats were forgotten. Fana understood that this was a very bad time for the family, which only the return of the menfolk could overcome.

When the spitting cobra came into the camp, Fana killed it. Everyone was very happy. They watched as Fana sat cross-legged on the bare ground and skinned the reptile. He cut all around the body immediately behind the crushed head, rolled the skin back, and peeled the tube of skin off the body. He handed the flesh to the women.

They laughed and took the snake. 'Yo, yo, yo, Fana, you are a hunter, you are a man, you have brought us meat.'

They cooked the snake and brought some meat to Fana. He shook his head.

'No,' he said, 'you need it,' he tapped his chest, 'for the babies.'

Grandfather, too, refused the meat.

Then the idea came to Fana. *I am a man-person*, he

thought, *a hunter. I brought this meat. I am a hunter. Therefore, I must hunt.*

It was still dark when Fana left the shelter the following morning. He remembered well what hunters carried when they went hunting. He took similar items; his small bow, a quiver of arrows, a short machete. He also had water in a stoppered ostrich eggshell, as well as his *kaross*, which he wore as a cloak. He did not see his mother's silent tears as he crept quietly into the pre-dawn darkness. She did not call him back. It was forbidden.

Fana slipped through the encampment, and when he was far enough away, he began to trot.

At first he followed the long disused game trail, but as the dawn broke, he swung off the faint path and ran in the direction of his shadow. Behind him, the great, round, red wound on the knee of the Hottentot god rose in the sky. Fana could feel its heat. When his shadow had shortened to only twice the length of his foot, Fana rested. In the shade of a low bush, he drank some water and ate a few dry berries he had found along the way. Small flies buzzed around him and he lazily swatted at them. Shadows disappeared as the Hottentot god strode past him, then lengthened back the way Fana had come. Now the wound on the Hottentot god's heel lit the world, as he strode across the earth towards the far horizon. Fana rose and followed him.

When the sun sank quickly towards the edge of the world, Fana looked for somewhere to spend the night. He climbed a tall thorn tree, nearly to the top, and settled into a narrow fork amongst the small, yellow flowers and brittle, green leaves in the umbrella-like canopy. As a precaution, he bound his body to the trunk of the tree with a leather thong. Then he slept.

Fana was woken by gentle sun kisses, filtering through the interlaced branches of the tree. He climbed halfway to the ground, then carefully inspected the dry landscape, before descending. He was thirsty, but there was little water left in the ostrich eggshell. Fana cast about until he found a line of short, green shoots poking out of the sand. He dug under the tallest shoots, grubbing out a narrow hole as deep as his arm was long. He waited as water slowly seeped into the bottom of the cavity. With a cupped hand, he scooped the water and dribbled it into the eggshell. When it was full, he replaced the stopper and drank from the well.

Fana found his shadow and began to follow it. As on the day before, he rested through the heat of noon, then followed the sun ever west-wards.

There was no tree to climb that night. The dry plain was dotted only with stunted bushes and drying aloes. Fana found a hole below the red tower of a crumbling, abandoned anthill, where an ant-bear had clawed his way into the next and used his long, sticky tongue to scoop up armies of ants.

For Fana, it was not a happy night. He dozed fitfully, waking to the cackling laugh of a hyena, the cough of a leopard. Once, hooves clattered past his hideaway, spraying sand on to his face. He gripped his machete tightly and shivered.

Well before daybreak burnished the horizon, Fana slid out of his burrow. Immediately he had left, a small snake shot out of the hole and slithered speedily away. Fana climbed to the top of the anthill, surveyed the horizon, turning full circle. In the distance, backlit by the falling moon, he could see tree-tops. He gathered his belongings and trotted towards the trees.

The sun was still clambering over the horizon when Fana crested the rise overlooking the glade. He saw them immediately. Elephants. A whole herd of elephants. Fana bent low and hid himself amongst the leaves and branches of a low bush. He watched the great animals for a long time. He thought of his father dancing the elephant dance, seeing in his mind the great ear, the long, sinuous trunk, comparing the imagined with the reality.

The thought of his father, the hunter, reminded Fana of his quest. Meat. Meat for his family, his group at the camp. There was a lot of meat here. Elephant meat. The idea did not shock Fana. It was the way life was lived. There was no choice. You killed and ate, or you died.

The only question Fana had to answer was how to kill an elephant. The answer came from Fana's Uncle Bayi. Sometimes, when Fana's father danced the elephant dance, Uncle Bayi would dance the elephant hunt dance. He danced the search for elephants, tracing the *spoor* in the dust with his fingers, so everybody present could see the exact size and shape of an elephant footprint. No detail was omitted. Here was a large bull, here a cow print; this one had limped on the back foot, this leaned on another leg. Here they rested, there they ran. He danced the sighting of the elephant herd, the hunter circling downwind, keeping out of sight of the great beasts. Yes, Fana remembered the entire dance. He knew exactly what to do.

Fana slipped back over the crest of the rise. He threw some dry vegetation into the air, watching to see the direction of the wind. Fana crept around the herd of elephants until he was downwind of them, then slowly stalked them. He came upon a great pile of elephant dung and, remembering, dropped his *kaross* in a thicket and smeared his entire naked body with the warm, pungent mess. This, he knew, would prevent the elephants from smelling his human scent, allowing him to get very close to them. He crept closer and closer, until he was amongst them. The elephants' rumbling stomachs sounded like thunder, the crackle of twigs in their churning maws like a fast-burning *veld* fire, the breaking branches and tree trunks snapping like lightning strikes, as the herd moved steadily through the glade.

Fana knew he must move quickly. He gripped his small machete tightly and ran up behind a smallish elephant. He slashed at the back of the animal's knees, desperately trying to cut through the hamstrings, so it couldn't run away. He swung again, but the machete hardly penetrated the thick skin. Again he tried, yet the sharp edge of the blade merely bounced off the elephant. Fana sweated, gasping for breath with the effort, sobbing in desperation. *This is the way*, he thought, *this is the way to hunt elephants. Uncle Bayi's dance told me, this is the way*!

A loud trumpeting sounded nearby. Fana looked around, saw a large elephant with great tusks moving towards him. He turned and ran, dropping his machete, desperately looking for somewhere to hide. The rolling thunder of the massive bulk of the elephant drummed closer behind him. Fana ran faster, his breaths burning his chest, his throat, great, gasping, searing gulps of air tearing into his body, as quickly expelled. The sharp, hot stones cut into his feet despite his hardened soles, and he felt every cut. His short legs stretched to longer strides than he had ever taken, his muscles burnt like fire, the bellows of his lungs fanning the blazing coals in his throat, his heart thundering, his head pounding and hammering as if it would burst. Then he tripped. Fana rolled in the dust as his entire world shook and shuddered.

The thunder stopped abruptly and immediately Fana found himself flying through the air, upwards towards the sun, so high he could feel the heat. He closed his eyes tightly, hoping the end would come quickly. He felt no sense of remorse, none of failure. It was a hunter's lot to fail often and succeed seldom. Fana descended fast. He could feel the approach of the ground, the hard, unyielding, bone-breaking, skull-smashing, rock-strewn earth.

Then he heard laughter, a chuckle rippling into full bloom. His father's laugh. As he opened his eyes, his falling body was caught and trapped by his father's arms.

'It is my boy,' the laughing voice called, 'it is my son, it is Fana.'

The other hunters of the clan came up to them. They giggled and whooped and touched Fana. Uncle Bayi took Fana and threw him in the air, catching him as Fana's father had done.

'He is a great hunter, our Fana,' Uncle Bayi shouted at the other men, 'he is a man now, he will be a bull elephant.' Bayi hooted with joy and pleasure.

Fana was tired, so Uncle Bayi carried him over his shoulder, easily maintaining the hunters' pace. In the distance, Fana could see the glade where he had hunted the elephants, but there was no sign of the massive animals there, nor on the open plain. When the hunters reached their camp, later the following day, Fana was saddened to see his grandfather was missing. And he knew for certain that his innocence and boyhood were gone when he saw his mother tending to his father's hunting wounds, her tongue clicking as she rubbed salve into the horizontal cuts and slashes behind his knees.

Peter's Puppy

Sandy Neville

It wasn't the scruffy, black dog that frightened Peter. No, it was the terrifying old woman who followed the dog. She wore dark, baggy clothes, and had straggly white hair.

The dog ran to the fence, barking. Peter backed away.

'What are you doing, boy?' the woman shouted. She had only one glittering, dark brown eye. Where her left eye should have been there was a ragged scar, running from her eyebrow down her cheek to the corner of her twisted mouth.

'I was only l-looking,' Peter stammered.

'Clear off.' She shook a bony first. 'You'll be sorry if I sees you round here again.' She didn't seem to have any teeth and globules of spit flew from her mouth as she shouted.

Peter turned and ran, crashing through thorny bushes and overhanging branches. He ran until he reached the gap in the hedge which led into Grandmother's garden.

He crawled back through the thick hedge, checking carefully that no one was around before emerging.

His thin arms and legs were covered in scratches,

some oozing blood. He found a screwed-up tissue in his pocket and dabbed at his injuries.

He was so engrossed that he didn't hear slow footsteps approaching.

'Whatever have you done?' Peter jumped when he heard Charlie's familiar voice.

'I caught myself on some bushes.'

'Looks to me like you've been in brambles.' Charlie's rough, sun-bronzed hand gently held Peter's arm. 'We'd best go to my shed and clean you up before Grandma sees you.'

Peter sat on a bench under the cobweb-strewn window. Dust particles danced in the sunbeams. The warm air inside the gardener's shed smelled comforting – a mixture of creosote, oil and pipe tobacco.

Charlie found a green first aid tin. Peter winced as the elderly gardener began cleaning his scratches with some antiseptic wipes.

'Some of these are deep,' said Charlie. 'You shouldn't go wandering about in the woods.'

'You won't tell Grandmother, will you, Charlie?' Peter asked anxiously. 'It's so boring having to stay in the garden.'

'It's none of my business what you do, young fella.' Charlie grunted as he bent to work on the wounds on Peter's legs. 'You'd best say you fell into the raspberries. That'll explain all these scratches.'

Peter nodded.

The old man slowly straightened up. 'There. That's better.'

'Thanks, Charlie.' Peter examined his arms and legs. There was now no blood to alarm Grandmother.

'So, what did you get up to in the woods?'

Peter fought back the temptation to tell Charlie about his hidden den.

'Nothing much,' he said quickly. 'I saw this house, with a thatched roof and lots of flowers in the garden. There were some puppies in a pen. I was looking at them when a strange woman shouted at me.'

'That'll be Mary Connolley. "Mad Mary" the kids call her. She's harmless enough.' Charlie grinned. 'She lost her eye in a terrible accident when she was young. She cares for sick animals. Prefers animals to people I reckon.'

The church clock chimed. 'You go in for your tea,' Charlie said. 'You don't want Grandma worrying any more than she does already.'

'I can't understand why you were near the raspberries,' Grandmother's bright blue eyes peered at Peter's arm. 'I should take you to see Dr Fairbrother. Those cuts could become infected.'

Peter swallowed his orange juice. 'Charlie cleaned them up properly,' he said. 'I'm sure they'll be OK.'

'Peter, dear, please don't say "OK". It's such a vulgar expression.'

'Sorry.' He took another sip of his drink.

'Grandmother.'

'Yes, dear.'

'May I go over to Joe's house tomorrow? He's got a new puppy.'

Grandmother's lips pursed and Peter knew what her answer would be. 'I'd rather you didn't, dear. Puppies carry diseases. I can't take chances, not with your asthma.'

Peter knew better than to protest.

'However,' Grandmother continued, 'I am working in the morning, but could take the afternoon off. Perhaps you'd like to go somewhere with me.'

'No, it's OK . . . all right, Grandmother, I'll stay here with Judith.' Judith, Charlie's wife, took care of the house while Grandmother was at work.

Grandmother looked disappointed and Peter felt almost sorry. Then she stiffened and said, 'Whatever you wish. You must please yourself.'

Peter waved Grandmother off and slowly walked back into the house.

He could hear Judith in the kitchen chatting to Charlie. 'He needs a bit of freedom, a boy of his age.'

Charlie's rumbling voice replied, 'It's hard on the lad, but he's all she's got now. After losing her only daughter that way, it's little wonder that she wraps the boy in cotton wool.'

Peter stood quietly in the dark hall. He knew they were talking about him. Peter's parents had been killed in a terrible fire when he was only a baby. He remembered nothing of them.

Grandmother loved him and everything she did was for his good, but he did wonder what life would be like if Mum and Dad were alive. Surely they wouldn't be as strict and fussy as Grandmother. Perhaps he'd have a pet of his own. He'd always wanted a dog, but Grandmother wouldn't allow it.

He walked towards the kitchen. Judith was still chattering as she unloaded the dishwasher. 'I still feel sorry for him – poor little beggar. . .'

Her voice tailed off as Peter stepped through the doorway.

Charlie looked across. 'How are your scratches?'

'Fine, thanks.' Peter was anxious to escape to the privacy of his den. He helped himself to an apple and said, 'I'll go out and play for a while.'

The sun was shinging brightly as Peter walked along the familiar rough path. The trees became thicker, blocking out the sunshine. He took a track, which led off the main path to a small brick building hidden behind a thick holly hedge.

The heavy wooden door was padlocked. Peter walked to the edge of the building and retrieved the key hidden under a large stone.

Inside his den it was warm and musty. The sun

streamed in through a glass panel in the roof. There was an old rug on the floor – Peter had found it at the back of Grandmother's garage. There was a box containing books and toys, which he'd smuggled from his bedroom. He sat on the rug, bit into his apple and picked up his latest *Harry Potter* book.

A few minutes passed when he heard a strange noise outside. He stopped reading and listened hard – nothing – he turned back to his book.

Now he was sure there was something out there. He heard a small whimpering sound.

Peter stood up. 'Who's there?' he called, his voice shaking. Everything went silent.

The boy quietly walked towards the door. He heard whining, coming from the holly hedge.

He crept over and then saw it. A small puppy, lying underneath the hedge, looking out with huge, frightened eyes.

'It's all right,' he said softly. 'I won't hurt you.'

He sat close to the puppy and slowly reached out. A small black nose twitched and then the puppy snarled. Peter could see tiny needle-sharp teeth. He held his hand still. Slowly, slowly the puppy's head moved forward until Peter could feel its breath on his hand.

The small animal stood. It moved closer. Its enormous, upright ears seemed too large for the small pointed face. It made a tiny snickering sound and rubbed against Peter's arm. The gold-brown fur was unbelievably soft and silky.

Peter gently stroked his new friend, tickling the white patch under its chin as the puppy emerged from its hiding place.

It was when he saw the white tip at the end of the bushy tail that Peter realised that this was no puppy but a fox cub. It was limping.

'You poor little thing,' murmured Peter.

It took a long time for Peter to persuade it to follow him through the doorway of his den. The cub limped across to the pool of sunlight on the rug and flopped down.

'I'll take care of you,' Peter said, as he too sat on the rug. 'You need a name . . . now let me see . . . yes, Holly. What do you think of that?'

The fox cub snickered again.

Now Peter began to worry. What did Holly eat? What was wrong with her leg? Questions and doubts flooded through his mind.

First, he must feed the cub. He was sure she was hungry.

'You stay here. I'll get some food,' he whispered. He left Holly dozing on the rug.

Holly's limp improved and she grew fatter over the next three days. All of Peter's time was now spent trying to slip away to the den, cleaning up after the cub and keeping her supplied with food and milk.

His money-box was almost empty. How was he going to feed Holly once his money ran out? He was already smuggling out pieces of sausage, ham and cheese from his own meals. Holly seemed to do nothing but eat and sleep. Peter couldn't imagine life without his fox cub. He loved her so much.

It was on Saturday morning that things started to go wrong.

'I thought we'd go away next week,' said Grandmother. 'I'll take a few days off. What about going to Cornwall? You loved it there last year.'

Peter's stomach flipped. He couldn't leave Holly, not even for one day. He stared blankly at his grandmother.

'Mmm,' was all he could manage.

'Goodness me. Don't sound so enthusiastic.' Her brow furrowed. 'We'll pack tomorrow and leave first thing on Monday.'

Peter ran to Charlie. Through tears, he told the old man about Holly.

'I can't leave her. She depends on me,' he sniffed.

Charlie gave him a handkerchief. 'You dry those tears and then take me to see Holly. I'll sort something out.'

Peter led the way to his secret hideaway. He unlocked the door.

Normally, Holly ran over to greet him but today she was slumped in a corner of the den. She'd been sick, very sick. The stench was overpowering.

Peter ran to the small cub. She could hardly lift her head. She was breathing fast and dribbling.

'Holly!' shrieked Peter. 'What's wrong?'

Charlie looked at the little cub, then he took off his jacket, lifted Holly gently from the floor, and wrapped her in the jacket.

'She needs help,' he said grimly, 'and there's only one person I know who can do anything for her.'

He hurried from the den, holding the sick cub to his chest. Peter ran behind.

The dog began barking as soon as Charlie rapped on the cottage door.

The green painted front door opened a crack.

'Who is it?'

'It's Charlie, Mary. I've got a sick fox cub.'

'Just a minute. I'll shut the dog away.'

Seconds later, the door opened. She looked even more frightening close up and Peter involuntarily backed away. She took no notice of him. She was looking at Holly and crooning softly to her.

'Come into the kitchen.' Mary led the way down a dark hall into a small kitchen. She washed her hands carefully and then examined Holly. The cub whimpered softly.

'What's she been eating?' Mary asked.

'P-p-puppy food and milk, mostly,' Peter replied.

'Too rich for a fox cub,' retorted Mary.

Peter's eyes filled with tears. It was his fault that Holly was so sick.

'Can you do anything for her?' Charlie asked, putting an arm around Peter's shoulders.

'I reckon I can,' said the old woman, stroking Holly's beautiful red-gold fur. She gave Peter a twisted smile.

'The little scrap would've died without you,' she said. 'You done your best. Now you leave her with me.'

Charlie began to head towards the door. 'Come on, young man.'

Peter sobbed as he tickled the top of Holly's head. 'Will I ever be able to have her back?'

Mary bent towards him. 'She's a wild creature and, though you love her, she's got to be allowed her freedom.' Her bony hand ruffled his hair. 'You can come and see her when you like. I'll get her fit and let her grow a bit, but then she must go free.'

Peter shook his head. 'But she could be killed or hurt. She's so little.'

'She'll be happier taking her chances in life, than being locked away.'

'Mary's right,' said Charlie. 'You think about it, Peter, and I know you'll agree.'

Tears streamed down Peter's face as he followed Charlie from the house.

When they arrived home, Charlie said, 'You go upstairs and tidy yourself up. I'm going to have a word with your grandma.'

The beautiful young vixen stared out of the pen and bared her teeth at Peter and his grandmother.

'I'm setting her free this evening,' said Mary. 'She's been penned up long enough.'

Holly looked sleek and fit. In only four weeks she had changed from a sick cub into a healthy, lively young fox.

'I'll put out food for a while,' Mary continued, 'but she'll soon be fending for herself.

Peter stared at Holly. She was now a wild fox. He could no longer stroke or tickle her as he had done during those few glorious days when he had thought she was his.

'Bye, Holly,' he whispered. Then he turned back towards the cottage.

'Can I go and see the puppies, please, Grandmother?'

'I'll come too, if I may,' Grandmother replied and she gave Mary a secret smile.

The four puppies waddled across, yipping and wagging their tiny upright tails as soon as they saw Peter. He knelt amongst them and they clambered over him.

Grandmother smiled down at her grandson. 'I think Mary's got something to tell you.'

Mary, too, smiled. Peter no longer noticed her scars. She was simply the kindest person he had ever known.

'I think you should have one of these puppies,' she said, 'and your grandmother agrees. So you choose one and in a week or so you can take it home with you.'

Peter stared in disbelief, his eyes shining with

happiness. He ran to Mary and hugged her and then he went over to Grandmother. 'Thank you,' he whispered.

'It's Charlie you should be thanking.' She kissed her grandson. 'He made me realise that by trying to protect you from life, I was making you miserable. All I want is for you to be happy.'

Peter hugged her. 'I am happy, Grandmother. So *very* happy.' He turned back towards the puppies.

Hiding Behind Suitcases

Ranaa Mirza Ahmed

How Luqmaan dreaded returning to school after the summer holidays.

The first thing Mrs Mitchell would ask for was a story titled 'What I did in the summer holidays'. Worse then writing it was being forced to read it aloud to the class. While the likes of Melody Trappes-Lomax boasted about the fun she had swimming with the dolphins in Florida, and Jason Goodman raved about the Niagara Falls, Luqmaan had to endure sniggers as he read out his accounts of pakora picnics in public parks and visits to the local museums and castles. Many of these tales of visits to local attractions with his cousins were not even true. Luqmaan's mother ran a busy post office so she didn't have the time to take him on many outings. The bit about cousins was a fib, too. Luqmaan had the misfortune of being the only Asian kid he knew that didn't belong to a big extended family – just his luck. Mum didn't have much family nearby and Dad, well, Mum didn't talk much about him but Luqmaan thought he must have been an only child like him.

Anyway, as far as holidays were concerned, things

were now looking up. Mum had just announced they were going on a 'proper' holiday next week.

'When you say "holiday", do you mean on an aeroplane and everything?' he asked his mum incredulously. Mum nodded, pleased to see him so happy.

'Are we going to America? Can we go to the Universal Film Studios?'

Mum shook her head.

'I know, I know!' Luqmaan squealed. 'We're going to see the pyramids in Egypt? The Alps in Switzerland? The Eiffel Tower in France? Or is it China to see the Great Wall?' Geography was definitely his favourite subject.

'Luqmaan, we're going to Pakistan.' He felt his face crumple.

'Pakistan! But that's a Third World country! Can we not go to India instead?' (Melody Trappes-Lomax had gone there last year to see the Taj Mahal so he reckoned India *must* be a cool place to go.) He could see Mum was disappointed by his reaction but all he could think of was the embarrassment of telling people at school that he went to Pakistan for his holiday.

'Yes, you are right, Luqmaan, there are lots of poor people in Pakistan, but there are also lots of good things about the place, too.'

'Like what?' he scowled.

'Well, like beautiful places to see, lots of cousins to play with, tasty food and nice sunny weather. Anyway, Granny is ill and wants to see you.'

'But I saw Granny yesterday and she was fine.'

'Not my mother,' said his mum quietly, 'your other granny.'

Well, that was that decided – arguing when a sick granny was involved was pointless.

One sulky week later, Luqmaan and his mum arrived at the airport for their holiday. Luqmaan had never seen so many Asian people before. There were hardly any in the town where he lived and at school there was only him and swotty Salma who was two years ahead of him, and also on a scholarship. Luqmaan stared at the queue ahead and behind him and wondered how all these people were going to fit on one plane.

Oh, no! He'd spotted Melody. Luqmaan huddled himself up on the baggage trolley and tried his best to hide behind his mum's large suitcase. Mum normally wore trousers but today, for some strange reason, she was wearing a shalwar kameeze – how embarrassing. She looked so traditional.

'What on earth are you doing, Luqmaan?' sighed his mum

'Need a rest, legs getting tired,' he mumbled, still keeping his head down. Luqmaan watched as Melody and her family moved on down the corridors of the airport till he could no longer see them. Lucky Mum had such a big suitcase.

It was time for Luqmaan and his mum to board the flight to Islamabad – the capital of Pakistan. He tried to act indifferent on the plane to show his mum he was still miffed about her choice of holiday destination. But he was so excited about being on an aeroplane for the first time that it was hard to look miserable, especially when he got to watch the latest instalment in the *Gary Trotter* film series. The journey was long and the novelty of looking down on tiny cars and tiny houses was wearing off. After picking at his tiny meal, Luqmaan eventually dozed off. . .

'Wake up darling, we've arrived.' A bleary eyed and dribbly Luqmaan awoke to hear his mother's voice. He felt like he had been sleeping for days. At first he wasn't sure where he was. His mum helped him up and they made their way to the door. Luqmaan was immediately met by a wall of heat. It was strangely comforting. They climbed the steps out of the plane, squinting in the bright sunlight.

This airport was very different to the one in Scotland. His mum looked nervously around at the crowds of people waiting to greet the passengers off the plane. Suddenly, a large woman came bounding up and flung her arms around Luqmaan's mum's neck. She was sobbing. His mum started sobbing too, and both women stood there hugging with their shoulders heaving. A confused and exhausted Luqmaan started to cry, too. Why was his mum crying? She must be upset about something. Why was he crying? – he wasn't a baby. He couldn't make sense of any of it.

'Don't cry, Luqmaan, this is my sister-in-law Ramessa. I'm just so happy to see her,' said Mum. Aunty Ramessa turned to Luqmaan.

'*Mashallah Farzana*, look how he's grown! Ten years ago when you first brought him here, he was just a tiny baby.' With that, she picked him up and started covering his face with kisses. Yuck! More people began to approach Luqmaan and his mum. There were a few wrinkly old ladies and some more chubby aunties like Aunty Ramessa; a couple of the ladies were holding babies. There were some older men who patted Luqmaan on the head as they greeted him and younger men who shook his hands. Luqmaan spotted a boy who looked about the same age as him. They both stared at each other curiously.

Luqmaan and his mum were then whisked away into the car park and a waiting car. He jumped with fright when he suddenly heard a tap at his window. He winced when he saw an old toothless man with only one arm staring in. The man kept repeating words that Luqmaan didn't understand. The uncle who was in the driver's seat rolled down his window and handed the man some money. Luqmaan looked at his mum for an explanation.

'He's a beggar, Luqmaan. He's asking for some money for food,' said his mum. Luqmaan reached into his rucksack and cautiously handed the man a melting chocolate cream egg and a carton of banana milkshake.

The car passed over lots of dusty, sandy, windy roads. Luqmaan began to experience sights he had never seen before. There were strange animals pulling carts; gigantic posters of the latest Bollywood films; cars that were not really cars but bikes with roofs; houses being built as houses were coming down. What a noisy place! He could hear car horns and loud music everywhere. Every now and then he would screw his nose up as a pongy smell wafted by. Luqmaan saw children playing on the dusty streets at every corner. Mum would never let him play outside with his friends so near the traffic, he thought to himself.

Finally, the car turned into a street of large white houses. This area was really pretty and peaceful. The houses looked beautiful and had colourful gardens. They reminded him of the villas he had seen on holiday programmes. The car drove into the drive of the grandest house of all. This, explained his mum, was Uncle Sikander's home and where they would be staying for the next two weeks. The boy he had seen at the airport came running out of the house and up to the car.

'Luqmaan, this is your cousin Adam,' said Uncle Sikander. 'You can play with each other tomorrow. Now it's time for you to rest after your journey.' Luqmaan and his mum were shown their room and within ten minutes they were both fast asleep. Luqmaan was having a wonderful, relaxing dream, when he suddenly awoke, terrified. It was dark and he couldn't see anything, but he could feel something moving on his head. He screamed for his mum.

'What's wrong, Luqmaan?' said his mum, anxiously turning on the light. Adam and his mum Aunty Ramessa came running into the room to see what the matter was.

'It's a lizard,' said Luqmaan's mum, picking up what looked like a miniature dinosaur. 'Don't worry, it won't hurt you, they are very common here.'

Adam started giggling hysterically. Aunty Ramessa glared at him. 'Don't laugh, poor Luqmaan, they don't have lizards in Scotland. It's not his fault he was frightened.' Adam was now laughing till the tears rolled down his cheeks.

Luqmaan was furious. How dare this silly boy make fun of him? He grabbed the lizard and hurled it at Adam. The lizard missed Adam and fell to the ground. To Luqmaan's utter horror, its tail came off. He felt sick; he hadn't meant to hurt it. All of a sudden the tail started moving and wandered off. Luqmaan stared in disbelief. 'It's not dead, it will grow again, that's what lizards do,' said his mum, as Aunty Ramessa picked up the creature and put it outside. Luqmaan could now see the funny side and he too started giggling with Adam.

The next morning, as he lay in bed, Luqmaan turned to face his mum in her bed at the opposite end of the room.

'Aunty Ramessa said I had been in Pakistan before,

but I don't remember, when was that?' he asked.

'You were just a few months old. It was nearly ten years ago,' said Mum, looking tense.

'Your dad. . .' she swallowed and paused. 'Your dad was very ill and he wasn't getting better, so he came here to see his family and . . . spend his last few days.'

'He died?' asked Luqmaan. His mum nodded nervously. She leapt out of the bed and picked up a framed photo from the dresser. 'Look, that's him,' she said, handing Luqmaan the picture. Luqmaan stared down and saw a man with a kind smiling face and curly hair holding a little baby. He looked a bit like Uncle Sikander. 'That's you and your dad, and that's me holding Adam,' she said, pointing at the woman in the picture.

'I'm so sorry I didn't tell you before. I didn't know how and it was easier to just not talk about it. I know it wasn't fair on you. Please forgive me,' said his mum. She looked like she might burst into tears at any moment. Luqmaan went running up to her and gave her a big hug. At last he had the answers he needed.

After breakfast, Luqmaan and his mum went to visit his dad's grave. It was covered in rose petals. His mum cried a lot, but she looked happy to be there. Luqmaan read a special prayer for his dad. They then went to visit Luqmaan's granny. *Imagine,* he thought to himself, *I'm going to meet Dad's mum.* She lived in a house not far from the graveyard, with her eldest son Jibriel. As Luqmaan entered the house he saw an old, thin, pale woman lying on a bed in the middle of the room. Without hesitation, he ran to her and held her hand.

'Luqmaan, you are here at last,' she whispered. Luqmaan did not know what to say, but he was happy to just sit on the bed beside her. She stroked his curly hair and smiled. 'Let's go and sit on the veranda,' she said, suddenly rising up out of the bed and on to her feet. She was wobbly so Luqmaan held her tight. Uncle Jibriel was amazed; 'She has not been out of bed for nearly three months.'

During his holiday, Luqmaan visited his granny most days and she began to get much better. 'You are the best medicine, Luqmaan,' she kept telling him.

Luqmaan and Adam had become inseparable. They did everything together. They flew kites from the roof tops, chased chickens in the courtyard, splashed in water, played computer games, watched the latest DVDs, went shopping in the bazaars and had fun in the many theme parks of Islamabad. It was brilliant having a cousin to play with, thought Luqmaan.

The holiday came to an end quickly. Too quickly, felt Luqmaan. The whole family came to see them off at the airport. Unlike when he had arrived two weeks earlier, this time Luqmaan knew why he was crying. He was crying out of sadness. He had never felt so loved in his life. He shared a special bond with these people and he was going to miss them. He didn't really want to leave them. Adam was the last to wish him farewell. The two boys hugged and then Adam pressed something into his hand. 'Look after Granny,' said Luqmaan. 'I'll email you,' he added as he as he waved goodbye.

As soon as Luqmaan got on the plane he unwrapped the gift that Adam had given him. He and his mum chuckled together. It was a small wooden carved lizard. He held it to his face and smelt it. Funny, but it smelt of Pakistan. Perhaps he would stick it on his bedroom ceiling just above his bed!

At the airport back in Scotland, Luqmaan couldn't wait to get home. How could he be so happy to be back when hours earlier he had been so sad to leave Pakistan? The holiday seemed like an amazing dream now he was back in familiar surroundings. He just wanted to go home, have a shower, eat a baked potato with beans and cheese, watch his favourite cartoon, and climb into his bed with the *Gary Trotter* bedcover. He might even start working on his 'What I did in the summer holidays' essay tonight. He couldn't wait to tell everyone about the striking scenery and the beautiful mosques, and the time he went to a place called Murree and caught the chairlift to the top of the snow-covered mountains. Perhaps he would also tell them about seeing his dad's grave and meeting his wonderful granny.

He beamed with pride as he caught sight of his reflection as he walked past a mirror in one of the airport shops. Didn't he look cool in his white linen embroidered shalwar kameeze?

Chiroptera

Vic McMaster

A long, long time ago, the animals of the Africa veld were not all as we know them today. The veld was the realm of the great spirit Omakaadu, who knows all things, and who sees all things, and who speaks in a voice of thunder. He generally allowed the birds and beasts of his realm to get on with life with little interference. But when things got really out of hand, he would sometimes intervene to restore the veld to its normal tranquillity.

Chiroptera was one of the animals that roamed the veld in those days. He looked not unlike a large gangly-legged dog with reddish-brown fur and tiny jet-black, bloodshot eyes. He had a lean and hungry look about him and, after a while, he became known as 'Chiroptera the Bad'.

The reason why he became known as 'Chiroptera the Bad' wasn't, as you may imagine, because of his unpleasant and unapproachable appearance, but because he had developed some rather nasty habits. It all started when he began slinking off on mysterious midnight trips into an unfriendly area of thick, overgrown bush that all other animals avoided. Animals would stay well clear of the area after dark and, in fact, even gave it a wide berth during daylight hours.

The area was known as the 'Valley of the Tokolosh'.

It was said to be a cold inhospitable place where the undergrowth was thick, and grotesquely twisted vines grasped upwards towards the dangling, tangled creepers above. The sun never penetrated the gloom of that place, where caverns entered deep under the earth, and where tortured and unearthly screams were said to rend the air at the end of night. A place where evil spirits were said to walk in the darkness. A place to send cold shivers up and down your spine.

Well, for some reason best known to himself – some said for sorcery and its evil rewards – Chiroptera took to visiting this unfriendly place every night, during the hours of darkness. After he had been engaged in these nightly activities for some time, the other animals began to notice that he had started to subtly change. They remarked that his small bloodshot eyes seemed to have become more sly and cunning and even more shifty than they had been before. He seemed to move with stealth he hadn't possessed before, and would creep up unnoticed, appearing suddenly out of nowhere. Other animals began to feel distinctly uncomfortable when he was about.

Then he started to approach some of the animals with strange and sinister requests. His requests only strengthened the belief that he was involved in sorcery and black magic. Most wanted nothing to do with him and did their best to avoid him wherever possible. But Chiroptera was wily and very hard to shake off, and he was certainly able to win over the hesitant or cautious with some very persuasive suggestions.

One morning, just as the sun made its appearance on the eastern horizon, Mhowani the Ostrich had a surprise visit from Chiroptera who sidled up to him and, peering round furtively, to make sure they were not overheard, whispered:

'Mhowani, I know all your innermost thoughts and desires. For example, I know that above all else, your greatest desire, and something you have never admitted to anyone else, is to have beautiful and elegant plumage. I know that you would dearly love to have long colourful feathers down the length of your fine wings and all down your long shapely legs. Glorious rainbow colours to match – no! Even to outshine – the peacock that you so envy.'

Mhowani was flabbergasted! How could Chiroptera have known about this, his one deep desire? Even though this creature repulsed him, he couldn't help himself – he had to know more. Chiroptera knew that he now had the vain bird's full and undivided attention. He went on; 'I, and I alone, can transform you into this beautiful creature. I have in my possession a most powerful potion, a potion with strong magical powers that will indeed transform you as I have described. However, I'm afraid you will have to wait until the night of the full moon. Immediately the moon rises in the sky you must carefully rub the potion into the full length of both your wings and, when that is done, generously apply the potion all over your legs. Within only two days, you will begin very quickly to develop the colourful plumage I have described, and you will be the envy of every bird in the veld.'

Chiroptera paused until he was sure that the big bird had time to picture himself fully in his mind's eye and was well and truly excited by the prospect of his new glorious plumage, before he allowed himself to continue.

'However, there is a price to pay for such fabulous potion. You will appreciate that nothing is just given away, especially nothing as valuable as my potion, without some sort of payment – and I'm afraid that in this case the price will be high.'

'Anything, anything within my power will be yours, if you can only give me the wonderful elixir,' blurted the excited ostrich.

Chiroptera's request was: 'You will bring me your mate's full clutch of eggs, for I have an urgent need for all of them! Then the potion will be yours.'

Mhowani was already shaking his head in disbelief, when Chiroptera quickly rushed on. 'It appears to be a fearful price to pay, I know, but think of it this way: You will be transformed very soon into the most beautiful creature in the veld. And next year, which isn't that far off, your mate can lay another clutch of eggs to replace this clutch. Just a relatively short delay to start a brood of chicks, whereas will you ever again be given a chance to outshine the peacock? – I think not!'

Eventually, after much thought and deep soul-searching, Mhowani gave way to vanity, just as Chiroptera knew he would, and the pact was sealed. How he managed to spirit away the clutch of eggs we shall never know, but this he did, and in return was given the ill-gotten potion. All he had to do now was wait until the night of the full moon.

The very next day, as the first rays of the sun turned the sky to gold, Chiroptera suddenly made his appearance at the sleeping-place of Gund'waan the Polecat.

'Gund'waan, my friend, I notice that you live alone,' said he. 'I also know that you lead a very lonely life, for you have but one friend, Pangolin the Scaly Anteater. And because I can look deeply into your soul, and know all your thoughts, I know that your one great desire is to be liked, to enjoy popularity and be the friend of all other animals.'

This was of course very true and Gund'waan was thunderstruck at Chiroptera's uncanny ability to look into his innermost yearnings. Chiroptera pressed on with his advantage.

'I have a mystic potion that could change your life by making you popular beyond your wildest dreams. You would become so popular that everyone, and I mean *every* living soul, would want to be your friend. This mystic potion I will give to you if you will simply do a small task for me.'

The excited little polecat, breathing rapidly with anticipation, breathlessly enquired, 'What must I do, what is this small task you need me to do in exchange for your mystic potion – tell me quickly!'

'On second thoughts, the price I ask may be just too high for one as timid as you,' mused Chiroptera, knowing full well that making the potion harder to obtain would serve to increase the polecat's resolve to acquire it.

'*ANYTHING*, anything, no matter how high the price, would I give for such a potion,' chittered the polecat.

'The price,' whispered Chiroptera, 'is a small portion of your friend, Pangolin's tail. At midnight tonight, when Pangolin is fast asleep, you will rub some ointment I will give you, on to the last two segments of your friend's tail. This will have the effect of numbing the area and your friend will not feel anything, as you cut through the flesh. You see, I desperately need the hindmost scales of an anteater's tail. I use them to make powerful magic.'

'But . . . but. . . He is my only friend,' whimpered the little polecat, 'how can I do such a thing to my friend?'

'I ask too much, this I know,' sighed Chiroptera. 'Ah, well. I did warn you that my price would be too high.'

He paused as if reconsidering, and only after some

time did he continue. 'On the other hand, you should nevertheless think about what is on offer to you. Pangolin surely cannot grudge a very small piece of his tail, and think of the offer you will be losing. You would be giving up the only opportunity of becoming the most popular animal, the very darling of the veld. For my part, I need these few scales to make powerful medicine to help others like you. Is this not a noble thing? Surely this is to the good of all concerned. Think deeply on it, my little friend, one swallow of my potion in the light of the full moon, and *viola!* What a charming and attractive chap I see – all the creatures of the veld, large and small, clamouring to be his friend. How happy he is, see how he smiles!'

Well, you can guess what reply Gund'waan gave Chiroptera in the end. Chiroptera dug around in his pouch and extracted some ointment to dull pain and a special sharp implement to be used to remove the end of the Pangolin's tail. He handed them to Gund'waan and then he quickly slipped away. Gund'waan waited tremblingly for nightfall and at midnight crept up to the sleeping Pangolin. He carefully rubbed the ointment on to the end of the anteater's tail. He then stopped, unable to carry on. He did his best to build up enough courage to deal with the next part of the foul deed. In the end he had to force himself to actually start cutting his friend's tail. Within a few minutes it was all over, and the anteater slumbered on, quite aware of his loss. Some time later, Gund'waan handed over his shameful spoils and, in return, received the coveted mystical potion.

When Pangolin awoke in the morning, he was aghast and mystified to find that the end of his tail had been roughly chopped off, leaving a bloody wound. He could not understand how this could have happened without his knowledge. He came to the conclusion that someone had done this to him while he slept. But who would do such a shameful thing? He was most dreadfully upset and was very ashamed of his disfigurement. The more he thought about it, the more certain he became that only one individual could have done this terrible thing to him. Only one animal knew the whereabouts of his sleeping place. The only one who could have done this horrible thing to him, was Gund'waan. Poor Pangolin, betrayed by his dearest friend? Pangolin did not wait to find out, but instead crept away into the deepest, darkest hole he could find. No longer would he mix with other animals, for fear of any further betrayal by those he had regarded as friends. And, to this day, he is seldom seen about in daylight.

Mhowani the Ostrich and Gund'waan the Polecat, in the meanwhile, with no regrets about the vile deeds they had so recently carried out, were both looking forward to the night of the full moon with eager anticipation. The days seemed to drag by, but at last the long-awaited night was upon them. As darkness fell, each in turn breathlessly watched for the first appearance of the full moon, and they were both armed with their potions. As the full orb of the moon rose majestically into the velvet sky, Mhowani carefully smeared the potion over the length of his wings and on to his legs, as Chiroptera had instructed.

While this was happening, another drama was unfolding in another part of the veld. In the bright moonlight, Gund'waan hastily gulped down the contents of the mystery potion also supplied by Chiroptera. At first nothing happened, but then Gund'waan felt a burning pain inside of him. The pain spread and grew more intense until, finally, Gund'waan lost consciousness and fell down in a deep faint.

Once Mhowani had completed smearing the potion on to his body he waited in anticipation for something wonderful to happen. He didn't have to wait long! He felt a searing pain wherever the potion had touched his skin. The pain grew worse, and increased to the point where Mhowani could bear the pain no longer and he collapsed unconscious to the ground.

When the first light of morning glowed red in the east, two sorry creatures awoke to find that something terrible had happened to them. Mhowani the Ostrich saw with horror that the feathers on his legs had shrivelled up and all but disappeared completely, leaving his long limbs bare and ugly. His large, sweeping wings had shrunk, and where they had once been were now two stubby little appendages, quite incapable of flight and utterly hopeless as wings. Gund'waan the Polecat opened his eyes and looked about him. How would it feel to be the most popular creature around, he wondered cheerfully. He felt and looked just the same as he always had, but what was that strange and sickening smell? After a while, and to his horror and disgust, Gund'waan slowly began to realise that the terrible odour was coming from his own body! No matter what he did he could not rid himself of the dreadful smell.

Chiroptera was well pleased with himself and gloated at the ease with which he had bamboozled the big bird and the polecat. All it had taken was a bit of planning and cunning and now he had got the items – the clutch of huge eggs and the anteater's scales – that he so dearly wanted and that would aid him in his dark sorcery and evil witchcraft. But his day of reckoning came sooner than he expected – in fact, that very same day.

Suddenly, the sky darkened as a big black cloud covered the sun and a mighty voice boomed out and was heard throughout the whole veld.

'Oh evil and wicked creature, you whom animals know as Chiroptera, I am the great wise spirit, I am Omakaadu and I know all things and I see all things and I speak with the voice of thunder.

'I have been watching you, Chiroptera, and your doings have greatly displeased me. Your vile and wicked ways, your sorcery and your meddling with my creatures have angered me greatly. You have changed the Ostrich who can now no longer glide on high with the eagle and the raven. You have changed him into an ungainly bird that will never fly again. Your meddling has shamed the Polecat into a lonely and miserable animal that will be shunned for all time by others for he carries a foul smell with him wherever he wanders. And my beautiful Pangolin has been reduced into a disfigured, shy and timid creature, who refuses to leave his dark burrow.

'I shall restore the Pangolin's tail to its original length, as he has done no harm to anyone. But the Ostrich and the Polecat shall remain as you have made them, as their punishment for their part in all of this. And henceforth the Polecat will be known by many as SKUNK and all will stay clear of the vile smelling creature.

'But on you, wicked Chiroptera, I will exact the greatest transformation. Because you used your sorcery on both animal and bird, you shall resemble a bit of both, but be neither one nor the other. You shall have wings, but no feathers. You will keep the face of the dog but will lose the legs of the dog. You will be reduced to scuttling along awkwardly on your belly. Never again will you hold your head up high but, in your ever-lasting shame, you will hang upside-down from your resting-place. Because you have carried out most of your evil work under the cloak of darkness, so from henceforward you shall live only in deep caverns and other dark places and will never again be seen in daylight. You will grow smaller and smaller until you are no bigger than a mouse. Your skin will become more leathery as you lose your fur. You will turn as black as the night creature you are.'

Immediately the great wise spirit Omakaadu finished speaking, a great bolt of lightning flashed down with a mighty crash of thunder. As the air cleared again, a small much transformed Chiroptera was to be seen. He was exactly as Omakaadu had said he would be. Some now call him Chiremwa-remwa but he is more generally known simply as '**bat**'.

The Trawler

Clive Bignell

The sun was warm when Lily emerged on deck. It was summer, the blue sky was dotted with the cleanest of clouds and the trawler, *Lily's Pad*, was making for home on a friendly sea. The young girl carried two mugs of tea and some toast on a tray to her father, who was stacking crates ready to be off loaded in Dartmouth. She loved mornings like this, having breakfast on deck as the gulls wheeled above their heads.

'Not before time, Lily love, did you sleep well?' He kissed her on the cheek as he took his breakfast. She nodded as she ate and gazed at the Start lighthouse. 'Have you finished your home work?'

She yawned and stretched, 'Yes, Dad.' She couldn't hide her lack of enthusiasm for another school day that was just beginning.

'What's up, Sweetpea, you like school, don't you?'

'I do, it's just, oh it doesn't matter.' And she threw a crust into the sky. Four seagulls dropped on to the toast squabbling.

'It's not those girls, again is it?' said her father, putting an arm around her as they watched the approaching land.

'Well, just the same one really.'

'And what has she been saying now?' His eyes were warm as he smiled down at her. 'Is she still making fun of you for living on a trawler?' He led her to the wheelhouse, and in his deepest pirate growl said, 'Take the wheel you scurvy dog, and don't put us on the rocks, or you'll walk the plank!'

She smiled as she took control of the small fishing trawler. A check of the seas all round revealed one other vessel, another trawler leaving the river. Not many boats were to be found out at this time of the morning. She was standing on a box at the wheel that lifted her high enough to see. Trawlers aren't designed to be steered by a nine year old.

'She's started calling me "little miss mackerel", says I smell of fish and I'm going to marry a haddock.'

'She's very silly, Lily.' And he smiled. 'You don't smell of fish because you shower and have clean clothes every morning, and your real name is Sweetpea and I've got my eye on a flounder for you to marry, but only when you're old enough!' Lily saw the twinkle in his eye as he gazed ahead and realised he was trying to cheer her up. She said nothing, but spun the wheel to starboard and headed for open sea.

'What's this, Shipmate, mutiny? I'll have you keel hauled, I'll feed you to the sharks, I'll send you to Davy Jones' locker. Now return to your course lest we lock you in a school for the rest of your days.' By this time, he was limping on an imaginary wooden leg, had a hump, and was whispering low and menacingly close.

'Oh, Dad, your breath stinks of marmalade,' and they both laughed as she brought *Lily's Pad* back on course.

'If it's too bad, Lily, I'll speak with your teachers.'

'No, Dad, don't you dare. She'll just be worse. I can put up with Barbie.'

Her father laughed, 'Why Barbie?'

'Her name's Cindy, it's just my little game.'

'You don't call her that to her face, do you? You'd be no better than her if you did.'

'No way. Bloomin' 'eck. She'd do her nut. But she *does* looks like a Barbie. Different fashions every day, latest trainers, fancy ringtone on her mobile. Her dad even drives a flashy pink Barbie car.'

'Well, if that's Cindy Moss you're talking about, her father's a very wealthy man. Unfortunately, wealth, good sense and taste don't always come together in the same box. It'll soon be the holidays love, and you can forget her.'

The thought of the holidays made Lily smile as she steered round the Checkstone buoy and entered the Dart. The swell died as they passed Dartmouth Castle and both were quiet until the tree-lined banks gave way to colourful houses. 'We could afford a small flat now, Lily, if you wanted to.'

'Don't you say that, I love this boat. I don't want to live in a little flat. I'm going to live on this boat for the rest of my life.'

'That's my girl,' smiled her father. 'Now, go and shower quick. We've got to leave in ten minutes.'

Within five, she had showered and was dressing in her own cabin. A bedroom like any other nine-year-old girl's, with posters on the walls, drawers full of hair brushes, bands and clips and a bed, hidden by cuddly toys. Only the round windows gave a clue you were on a boat. Her father had decided two years earlier when her mother died that, rather than have help to look after Lily, he would fish during the night while she slept below and, while she was at school, he would shop, clean and wash their clothes.

'Come on, Sweetpea, time to go.'

She rushed up on deck still brushing her hair. Her father, already sitting in the open truck, had the engine running. She climbed the vertical steps, swung her bag into the back, amongst the fishing gear, and jumped in. 'To school Cap'n, and don't spare the horses.'

He laughed out loud as the truck tyres squealed, just a little, and they drove from the harbour.

Cindy Moss had been a nightmare those last days of term. She sneered, boasted and her taunting of Lily was non-stop. At one point, she even called her a fairy. Her, Lily Ryder, part-time trawler skipper! A fairy? What was she on?

That was in the past now. A week ago, the gate had

opened early, and the inmates had poured through, their sentence served and freedom assured for seven weeks. Lily hadn't thought about Cindy for days now. She was at that moment steering for the river entrance, while her father tied down crates. The trawler was pitching around in a windswept sea, heading for home.

He appeared at the wheelhouse door. 'I shan't be sorry to get out of this, Shipmate.' He smiled, seawater running off his head on to yellow oilskins.

A few miles out, rain was already falling on to an angry sea dotted with whitecaps and the southerly wind was driving it towards them. The trawler was built for these seas and worse, but her father didn't want Lily out in storms if it could be avoided.

Heavy seas followed them into the river, crashing on to rocks and turning to foam. Only after they passed Warfleet did the swell subside and Lily relaxed on the wheel. It was then they saw the white motor yacht coming towards them.

Her father reached for the radio and turned to channel sixteen while reading the name of the yacht as it passed.

'Calling *Mosaic*, this is *Lily's Pad*, do you read me, over?' He switched to receive, and after a few seconds of crackling, a well-to-do voice filled the wheelhouse.

'This is *Mosaic*. What do you want, over?'

He didn't like the man's tone, but spoke again. '*Mosaic*, we're the trawler you've just passed, and I thought I'd let you know it's rough out there and getting worse, over.'

Again the same voice. 'Not that it's any of your business, but we're only going to Brixham for dinner. Over and out!' With that, the crackling returned.

'They'll bounce around like a cork in that boat. I hope their stomachs are strong enough for food when they get there.' He disappeared on to deck. The helmsman on the lower ferry saluted Lily as they passed, and she smiled and saluted back.

Twenty minutes later, her father was delivering fish to various hotels and restaurants and Lily was reading on her bunk. She heard the radio crackle and then the word 'Mayday'. She ran to the wheelhouse.

Again the crackle and then, 'Mayday. This is the *Mosaic*. Our engines have failed and we're drifting towards the rocks. Can anyone hear me, over?' Lily could hear the panic in the man's voice and instinctively snatched up the handset.

'*Mosaic*, this is *Lily's Pad*. What is your position, over?'

The voice came back. 'But you're . . . you're a child! Clear the lines, I haven't got long.'

'This is *Lily's Pad,* I will get you help immediately, but I need your position. Can you see the "Mewstone", over?'

'Yes, yes, about half a mile from hitting it. Call the coastguard, but for God's sake be quick,' and then Lily heard him say 'It's only a girl' to someone with him.

'*Mosaic*, this is *Lily's Pad*, I am dialling for help on my mobile as I speak. You must drop your anchor and all of your chain. That should delay your drift. Over and out.'

'Emergency services, which service, please?' The connection was quick.

'Coastguard, please. Yacht in trouble at mouth of Dartmouth Harbour.'

Again the connection was immediate. 'Coastguard, can I have your name and telephone number, please?' Lily give the information. 'How can we help?'

'Did you pick up the Mayday from *Mosaic*?'

'We did. The lifeboat's out on a shout already so we're putting out a Pan-Pan at the moment. Thank you for your call.'

By the time the call finished, the trawler's engine was already growling. Lily knew that a Pan-Pan was a call to all boats in the area to give assistance to a stricken vessel. She also knew that, apart from *Mosaic*, she'd seen no other boats out there. Within seconds, she was on deck dropping the lines and powering away from the quay. She was working on automatic now. The lifeboat was on another mission. No other boats were close. Her father was at least an hour from returning. It was down to her.

She didn't see the ferryman wave this time as the trawler ploughed her way towards the river entrance and the darkest of grey clouds. As they passed 'One Gun Point', the seas began to build and the rain spattered the screen.

'*Mosaic*, this is *Lily's Pad*. The lifeboat is on its way, but might be a while. I'm coming to help if I can, over.'

'Good lord, you're a child, what can you do?' The voice was becoming more and more strained.

'*Mosaic*, have you dropped your anchor, over?'

'Yes, yes, but it's dragging.' The voice was shouting now.

'*Mosaic*, if you get to within fifty metres start to draw in your chain slowly and have a boat hook ready, over and out.' As the trawler fought her way towards the headland, Lily pulled on her oilskins and boots and attached her lifeline.

Time dragged as the trawler crashed into trough after trough, but finally Lily saw *Mosaic* as she rounded West Rock, still rising and falling to each spray-topped wave that drove through.

'*Mosaic*, I am going to your bow and will throw a float with line attached. Draw the line in and a rope will follow. Tie it to your bow, over.'

'Yes, but hurry . . . hurry!' the man was crying now as he shouted. 'I have children aboard!' He seemed to forget that he was talking to a child.

I hope he's up to this, thought Lily, as she steered the squat trawler at the white and chrome yacht. At the last moment, she swung her boat to starboard and slowed the engines. Only now could she see how big the swell was. The two boats were rising and falling on different waves, towering above each other in turn. She knew they only had seconds.

She grabbed the line she'd prepared and plunged through the door on to a heaving deck awash with water. Wind and rain drummed the hood of her oilskins as she clipped herself to a strong point on the cabin and looked back. She saw the man already at the bows, no waterproofs, clutching to the rolling deck. Behind him, a plume of spray exploded from the Mewstone. This throw had better be good.

She tied the trailing end of the thin line to her wrist and loosened the coils ready for throwing. The trawler had now begun to drift towards the yacht, whose anchor was gripping at that moment. They would soon collide. She hurled the float and line out into the stormy sky, where it caught the wind and arced towards the yacht. Luck was with them. The float skidded across the deck of *Mosaic*, trailing the line over the guard rails. *Even he should get that*, thought Lily, as she tied the line to the strongest warp and fed it out. It was too heavy for a child to throw over.

She raced back into the wheelhouse, unclipping the lifeline as she went, and slammed the door. With a glance, she saw the man slipping his way back to his cabin and the warp fixed to his bow. She gunned the engine and immediately the trawler began to make ground. As the last of the warp fed over the side, she cut the engine until the tension was taken and then eased her forward again, and not before time.

At that moment, the dingy hanging from the yacht's stern smashed on to the first of the rocks and was crushed like paper. They began, slowly at first, to pull away from the rocks. Lily could feel the extra load on the trawler and had to be careful not to break the towline. Metre by metre they edged away from danger like two carriages on a massive rollercoaster, punching into the storm.

'*Mosaic*, haul in the rest of your anchor now, over,' and she watched as it cleared the water. After they had gained about a hundred metres, Lily turned to starboard to run with the wind on her side instead of fighting against it. She knew now that the worst was over and as long as she protected the warp, all would be fine. A shiver ran through her body. Was that nerves or the cold? *It must be the cold*, thought Lily, and smiled to herself.

The radio crackled, 'You've done a fine job young lady, you will be well rewarded for this.' He sounded a little calmer now, but still full of emotion. 'Tell me, my daughter Cindy wants to know, are you Lily Ryder, over?'

She looked behind her at the yacht as it rode the green swell and the word *Mosaic* painted on her bows. It was spelt with a double 's'. Moss . . . aic. Cindy Moss. She couldn't believe it.

As she turned the trawler towards the safety of Dartmouth Harbour, she lifted the handset. '*Mosaic,* this *is* Lily Ryder, I hope you're all OK, over,' and as she returned the handset to its cradle she smiled and said, to no one in particular, 'Who's a fairy now, eh!'

The Baker's Boy

Adrian Burice

Not so long ago, there was once a country whose name is now remembered only in books. The books tell of a war and of how this country was cut up into slices like a cake and of how greedy men re-named these slices of cake. In this country, while it was still a whole cake, there was a village with a church, a bakery, a cafe in a square and a river with a stone bridge over it.

At the time of the war, in this village there was a baker's boy who delivered fat golden loaves and small plump rolls from the basket of a black bicycle. He criss-crossed the cat's cradle of roads that linked the houses and shops and bound them tight to the yellow stone church. Cycling toughened his leg muscles, making them elastic as rubber, so that he always made the junior football team. They played most weekends on their pitch across the river on the edge of the pine forest.

The war started in the summer. He heard the men talk about nothing else at the cafe tables in the square. They drank bitter coffee, sucked on strong pipe tobacco and bit fiercely into the pastries he delivered. Sometimes, they went inside to watch news of the war on the television mounted in a gloomy corner above the crates of beer and wine bottles. There the boy saw pictures of aeroplanes and tanks and rows of men with their hands raised in surrender.

The women talked of the war across their gardens and lines of washing. They came out to take their bread orders and to pay their bills grudgingly. The paper money they gave him was greasy, as if it had been soaked in olive oil. The women feared for their sons, who were sitting down in the cafe on the square. 'You,' they would say accusingly, 'are lucky. Why? Because you are too young to be taken.'

He had no opinion about the war. He did not even know who the enemy was. A bomb dropped from an aeroplane and demolished the church tower. The golden bell lay crackled in pieces in the square for days, and the pink tiles were scattered about the square and down the damp side-streets like autumn leaves.

He had no opinion about the war, not even when the price of flour rose again and again, and the baker raised his bread prices again and again. People suspected that he put up his prices simply to make more money and this may have been true. Certainly, he grew fatter, smoked larger cigars and his wife bought a new coat for the winter when most people hadn't enough money even to buy food.

But then his father joined the army. That autumn, the town lost its men as the trees lost their leaves. His mother cried upstairs for a long time and then went mad, cleaning the whole house from top to bottom. The baker's boy got clouted for treading dirt into the immaculate kitchen. He went outside and kicked his bike over because there were no younger brothers or sisters to take his anger out on.

In November, the bread was rationed. The women handed over papers like raffle tickets along with the ever increasing bundles of banknotes.

The football pitch by the pine forest was fenced in to contain ten wooden prison huts.

One day, the prisoners arrived. They came like a slow, grey train, marching through the town in pairs, their legs shackled with black chains. Their heads were shaved white, dirtied round the sides with stubble.

A soldier carrying a rifle stopped the baker's boy at the bridge to let the prisoners pass over.

The prisoners marched by with their heads bent. Their leg-chains rattled on the wet cobbles. One man slipped and fell to his knees. The baker's boy stooped to help him and straightaway felt the butt of the solder's rifle jam into his ribs. 'You leave him, boy,' he barked.

The prisoner got to his feet, looked long at the baker's boy and then walked on. The boy looked long at the numbers on the prisoner's back as if they were a sum to be solved on the school blackboard.

It snowed all the rest of the day and the night, too. So that in the morning, the baker's boy lifted the wooden sledge down from its iron hooks in the barn. He cleaned off the rust from the runners and rubbed them with candle wax until they were both smooth and gleamed silver like swords. For the next three months this was the only way to deliver the village bread: from a big wicker basket strapped to his sledge with yellow rope.

Because he bribed the guards, the baker won the contract to supply the prison with bread. He rubbed his hands together and tugged the pencil out from behind his sweaty ear. Then he began to work out his profits on the back of a bread bag. The baker's boy noticed how the baker used poor grade flour for the prisoners' bread and mixed in plaster dust from the bakery floor to make the dough go further.

One day, when the baker was over in the cafe, calculating his profits and drinking brandy, the van came for the prison bread. The driver shooed a prisoner in to do the carrying while he sat in a chair tucking into fresh bread smeared with golden butter. The prisoner grinned at the boy. It was the same prisoner who had stumbled on the bridge. The baker's boy smiled back and then bit his lip. This man was the Enemy, for heaven's sake, he had to remind himself. The driver sat by the oven, warming his hands and dozing into a sleep.

The prisoner shuffled to and fro with racks of the grey bread. Not one could he steal because each one was accounted for on the baker's bill. Counting had made the baker a wealthy man. So, the baker's boy unthinkingly went up to the prisoner, made sure no one saw, and pushed a golden, plump loaf under the man's prison tunic. The loaf was meant for the hotel where the generals stayed. The man smiled.

And so there began a new pattern in the boy's life. In addition to criss-crossing the town, he was double-crossing the baker. At each bread collection he would slip the prisoner some bread. One time, he gave him a flour sack, cut down one edge to make a hood against the snow that blew horizontally down the mountains and into the valley where the town was. Another time, he gave him cloth to bind his feet and he gasped at the blue colour of the man's toes, the flesh swollen and bloody with chilblains. Yet another time, he gave him a pencil stub and some paper.

At Christmas, he gave him four squares of Swiss chocolate wrapped in a sheet of newspaper.

They never spoke. Their silence was not maintained out of respect for the dozy guard. It was because neither man nor boy spoke the other's language.

So the winter of silences and deception wore on. Children skated under the bridge on the frozen mirror of the river as they had always done. Snow hung in creamy dollops from the branches of the trees in the pine forest as it had always done. Icicles grew into crystal daggers from the eaves of the houses as they had done since the first house had been built in the valley centuries ago. Boys threw snowballs at the icicles to knock them down and enjoy the music of their breaking as their fathers had done before them and their fathers before them. The baker's boy was doing this when his mother called him into the kitchen.

She had been crying and her face was white as the snow except for her nose, which was red as a holly berry. She showed him the letter, which said that his father was 'missing in action, presumed dead'. He went to the framed photograph of his father on the dresser and asked his mother the dreaded question: 'Does that mean we will never see him again, Mother?' His mother nodded and then she bitterly cursed the war and the enemies who had robbed her of her man.

The baker's boy went to be by himself in the barn. He sat down on his sledge and felt the wooden grain with his fingers. He looked up at the chisels and saws that his father had used for building his sledge. It was then that he made a vow. He breathed it into the freezing air, solemnly as if this was a church and his sledge an altar, and he crossed his heart and hoped to die if ever he broke it.

The next time the van called for prison bread the baker's boy was ready. The prisoner looked in vain for his little friend. So he was taken by surprise when an icy snowball struck him full on the nose. Tracks of blood dripped down his lip and dotted the trodden snow. The guard laughed at the boy and called out: 'That's the way to treat the enemy, my boy.'

From that day, the baker's boy never gave the prisoner a thing. Unless you counted as gifts the icy snowballs, the chunks of ice and lumps of mouldy dough that thudded against the numbers on his back.

And people were quick to note a change in the baker's boy. He missed school, choosing the company of boys who passed the day smoking under the bridge and shouting out rude words to the girls who crossed the river to work in the tank factory in the pine forest. He learned to swear and his mother did not know what to do with him so she hit him with her biggest spoon. He learned to cheat both the baker and his customers out of their greasy bank notes. He walked about jauntily, touring the town with his hands thrust in his pockets and a toothy grin on his silly face. In short, he was miserable.

Spring came slowly that year. Some of the baker's boy's customers said it would never come. They called it an omen. But that was just old folks' talk. For come it did. By degrees, the river unfroze and gushed brown and green water that came from the melting snows of the mountains.

First there were snowdrops, tiny young things mad to be out in the cold, and then the green spears of daffodils thrust up through the soil. The trees budded little green fists. The days were longer and the baker's boy was home before dark.

And all this time, he never broke his vow that he had made over his father's sledge. Even the guards, rough men with grating voices, thought he took the torment of the prisoner too far. They drove him away with their rifle butts. Finally, a guard struck him down, sickened by his taunting of the prisoner.

The baker's boy sloped home like a kicked dog. He wheeled his delivery bicycle with one hand and nursed his swollen eye with the other. His mother was in the kitchen, sitting at the table in front of a square of paper. He hoped to avoid her but she caught his hand and made him sit down. Then she showed him the letter, which said a lot of official things in typewriting. But among all the words was the message which made his heart beat until he thought it would burst. His father. The great sledge builder of the town was alive and well, but a prisoner-of-war in a camp for captured soldiers on the edge of a pine forest in another country.

★

His sleep that night was for once unbroken by dreams. He woke early. The sun warmed his back and he smelled the bread on the air long before he reached the bakery. He loaded up the basket with its cargo of loaves. They were hot like bricks in a summer sun.

By the bridge, he left the bicycle and chose the biggest loaf from the basket. Then he walked beside the sparkling river until he came to the pine forest and the prison camp. At each corner of the camp there was a wooden turret topped by a manned machine gun. He continued along the path that ran beside the fence. He looked anxiously at each hut.

Prisoners, all dressed in the same grey prison tunic,

tumbled down the steps of each hut, called to the parade ground by a hooter.

The baker's boy stopped by the last hut and watched it empty itself of men. A silence grew as their voices shrank away. He heard the first skylark of the year sing somewhere. Then came footsteps. A man came carefully down the wooden steps of the hut. He moved slowly as if he had been sick and each footstep hurt.

The baker's boy placed a hand on the wire and whistled to the prisoner. He knew it was his prisoner by the numbers on his back. The man looked at him hard and then turned away. He started to walk. His feet shuffled in the dry dirt.

Then the baker's boy drew back his arm and hurled the golden loaf of bread with all his might. It flew into the air and fell in an arc over the fence, thudding into the man's back right where the numbers were. The prisoner faltered, turned and fell to his knees before the bread. He broke the bread, stuffed some into his mouth and then laughed. The laugh was long and deep. It was like a wind rippling along a forest path. It was like the echo at the bottom of an oak barrel and it went on and on. Suddenly, the prisoner tucked the loaf under his jacket, waved to the boy and skipped away after his fellow prisoners. The baker's boy watched him go. Then he ran back to his bicycle and pedalled away hard over the bridge and up towards the church.

So it was that the baker's boy began to give bread

once more to his prisoner and with the giving his hope for his own father grew and grew until it could not help but come true . . .

Somewhere, at the edge of another pine forest in another country a boy he could not talk to was giving bread to another prisoner.

The Antibody Kids

Tim Holmes

Eight children had been taken. All but one had been brought back. Right now, Karl Graham was still trapped in a world partly of his own making, a place that a courageous brother and sister would have to enter to bring him home.

Laura Jericho paced the cluttered office, stepping over piles of books and notes, while her brother Peter perched nervously on the edge of a chair, knowing that the time would again come for them to willingly infect themselves with the virus.

'Let's go over this again,' said Laura in her commanding voice. 'We've been able to bring the others back but not Karl, why not?'

'For the thirteenth time and counting, I don't know, Sis,' replied Peter. 'We did the same for Karl as we did for everyone else, but he didn't believe us, so he stayed.'

'Exactly! He didn't believe us, he thinks that he lives there.'

'Yeah, he really believes he's Prince Particular of the Northern Peninsular.' Peter hid his amusement by taking a sip from a can of drink.

Laura studied the various piles of possessions stacked upon file cabinets; countless tales from Karl's childhood swimming around in her head. Would it be a name or the detail of a story that would bring Karl back?

'We've got to get him this time,' said Laura quietly but firmly to Peter, her voice almost dropping to a whisper, 'otherwise he might never come back and we've failed.'

As they opened the door of the office, a wave of voices and commotion swept in. Laura and Peter turned into a bright corridor lined with guards in blue uniform. They were there to keep reporters away from them. Their destination was the door at the far end where a short tubby man in a long white coat and glasses awaited them.

'Are you all set?' said the man in a nervous trembling voice. 'Remember, it took two trips to bring little Katie back . . . I'm confident. . .'

The children passed through the door behind the man without saying a word. They entered the main control area, from which the whole operation was supervised; a room stacked with screens, keyboards and cables criss-crossing over everything. Through glass panels Karl could be seen seated in a chair, connected up to machines that monitored his heart rate and brain activity, his icy blue eyes wide open.

Laura and Peter were handed facemasks to wear and then escorted into the dimly lit main chamber and seated beside Karl. They too were attached to the monitoring equipment. Peter watched the men in their protective suits exit the chamber and wondered why it was that no adult had even caught this illness. Surely they had initially breathed the air of the infected children when they had found them, seated in a circle, staring into nothingness.

A distorted voice entered the room. 'Everything is in the green here,' a hesitant pause, 'you may remove the masks in your own time.'

This was the strangest part of the process. Laura and Peter held hands and removed the masks with the other; it would take a minute or so until the effects took hold. The important thing now was to remember that the world they were about to enter was not real, but one maintained by the virus and Karl's imagination. If they were to forget this, then their own minds would be taken and all three of them might never return.

'Good luck,' came the distorted voice from the control room.

Laura underwent the effects first. The drone of the equipment around her dissolved and all that could be heard was a gentle continuous echoing thud. Then the muscles started to fully relax, her hand slipping from Peter's and she was unable to move at all, not even so much as a blink. Helplessness. Laura could only stare forward at the scientists through the panels in front of her. This image then started to move quickly away, as if she were hurtling backwards down a tunnel at hundreds of miles per hour, while the thudding sound became louder and more frequent. Her vision was now fast becoming no more than a single faint dot at the centre of complete blackness. She felt as if she was leaving her body completely. Then – nothing.

Laura's hearing and vision came back in an instant. She was lying face down in the warm grass. As she rose, Peter appeared, propped up against a tree trunk, shaking his head.

'We made it, Peter, this is not real!'

'I know, are you OK, Sis?' replied her brother, struggling to his feet.

She ignored him. Something else occupied her attention. From a large opening in the ground, a waterfall cascaded up into the air. Reflecting the rich purples and blues of the night, it flowed far into the heavens triggering ripples that erupted out miles across the sky. *This could not be real,* thought Laura, but it always felt like it was.

'Well, that's new,' said Peter. 'If I had been stuck here, I wonder if my imagination would have come up with one of those?'

'There's been quite a few changes since last time,' said Laura, as she strode out away from the forest to take a better look around the area. The vast green terrain was no longer flat, but peaked up into hills to the east and west and then dipped sharply towards the dark blue ocean to the south.

Laura knelt and examined the knee-high grass as it gently swayed back and forth. Her head suddenly snapped back towards her brother. 'Karl had an argument with his brother before he came here, we must try to remind him, it could be the breakthrough.'

'OK, Sis . . . hey, check that out,' shouted Peter excitedly. Laura craned her head up to see an immense sailing-ship gliding silently overhead. On each side, colossal wings flapped occasionally to keep the vessel buoyant on the warm gentle night-time breeze. Alongside it, ten or more smaller ships darted to and fro with wings that beat so fast they were almost invisible. The crafts gradually moved into silhouette as the giant moon, low in the sky over the southern ocean, became their backdrop.

'That is the 23rd Squadron, it is to join the rest of the fleet for the parade at dawn,' pronounced a clear, confident voice. A small figure looked down from atop a proud black stallion and quickly dismounted, dropping next to them. He was roughly the same size as Laura and Peter, his dazzling blond hair shining brightly. 'I did wonder if I would ever see you two here again, how do you like the changes?'

Laura spoke up. 'Karl, this place, it's not real. Come back home.'

'Must we go through this again?' said Karl. 'At least let us dine before you say what you clearly feel you have to, and I would prefer to be referred to as majesty.'

'The longer you stay here, the stronger the virus gets,' started Peter, 'if you can try to remember your real home, all this will just disappear.'

Karl slowly ambled over to his horse and patted him on the side; the animal shook its head in approval and looked away to inspect a herd of deer-like animals charging across the horizon to the east. Karl turned back towards them and sighed. 'Why would I want to leave here? It's perfect, it's paradise.'

'Your family and friends miss you. Your brother misses you.' Laura spoke slowly, 'You had a row with him, can you remember that, Karl?'

Karl gestured towards his horse, 'Risvu is my friend and my brother, he and I are together all the time.'

Peter looked away from the boy and noticed a ship, much like the smaller vessels that flanked the 23rd Squadron, heading down towards them. Karl's face lit up when he saw it. 'I shall be taking a short trip to inspect my kingdom, would you care to join me?'

The ship landed and Risvu cantered over to the side of the hull. As Karl approached, the animal rose high up on to its hind legs and opened the side of the vehicle with its front hooves. Laura, who had been watching the creature with interest for a while, followed closely. Peter advanced cautiously, never taking his eyes off the horse as he entered. The passengers took up their places on opposite sides of the ship, while Risvu stood at the side staring out.

'As you can see, this vehicle is different from those in my fleet, it is kept aloft by the balloon.' He signalled up towards the stretched inflatable attached by cables at each corner, 'It is so much more preferable to those unsightly wings on my armoured division.'

Karl then produced a small item from around his neck and blew into it. Laura and Peter watched fascinated as a large flock of doves rose from a forest in the west and travelled towards them. The birds hovered behind the balloon, tilting so their undersides faced the ship, and beat their wings violently. The force of the wind created sent the vessel soaring high up into the skies.

The craft drifted leisurely over towards the north of the kingdom; enormous cragged snow-capped mountains passing below. Suddenly, Peter sat up as he become aware of a strange sound. There seemed to be musical tones originating from beneath them, each a good thirty seconds apart, and every now and then a note so low in pitch, that it could actually be felt in the stomach.

'Are those mountains singing?' said Peter, bemused.

'Indeed, sometimes they sing me to sleep, I find their music very relaxing.'

Suddenly Laura spoke. 'It's you! You're the virus!'

A puzzled Karl was about to speak up; when to his utter astonishment and Peter's too, Risvu turned back towards them and answered her, his deep booming voice matching the magnificence of his form.

'I am glad you understand now.'

Laura marched towards the animal. 'When Peter and I came here for the others, they always had someone with them, a close friend.'

Risvu turned away from her and looked out over the land. 'That's right, we like to keep an eye on our most precious individuals.'

'Why did you bring them here?' asked Laura. Her brother sat open-mouthed, this easily beat the winged ships.

'It is children who control this land, without them we might slowly fade away. If only you could see all of the wonderful things they have created in their short time here.'

Karl listened attentively, his mind performing cartwheels to keep up with the new information. Risvu continued. 'As children grow into adults they lose the purity of the imagination, they question too much. For the young, life is an adventure; anything seems possible in their imagination. As you have seen, anything *is* possible here in the imagination.'

'Are you saying my kingdom isn't real? You mean this isn't my real home?' said Karl, tears forming in his eyes.

'This can be real any time, if you really want it to be,' said Risvu calmly, as he pointed out with his head to another majestic sky waterfall nearby.

'But you knew that Karl, Katie and the others had

families and you were keeping them apart,' said Laura.

'We only brought them here temporarily. They were to be messengers of this world, a place that adults and even some children are beginning to ignore. We knew that you would come eventually to take them back.'

Peter had just about recovered from the shock of a talking horse. 'I don't quite . . . follow . . . a lot of things actually.'

'We had the power to bring them here you see, but not to send them home. That was to be your job; to remind them of their homes, families and friends, and lead them back.'

Laura spoke out angrily. 'Do you realise what pain you've put their families through?'

Risvu looked down in shame. 'I apologise, we did not know of any other way. Although think, right now, the children who have visited will be talking about us. Books will most certainly be written and read about this world of the mind. Every girl and boy, man and woman, has the power of the imagination, and may travel into it any time they choose. Never forget this.'

Risvu looked in the direction of the weeping boy. 'I think it is time for you to return, Karl.'

'But I cannot remember my home, how do I get back?' he yelled at the top of his voice.

The four children remained still and quiet, passing lakes and forests, the bizarre animal life scattering as the balloon passed overhead. Then Peter stood up, walked to the edge of the ship and pointed out in the direction of the distant ocean, its waters glittering under the light of the moon. 'The Lake of Ukulele. You and your father drive there every weekend to go fishing.'

Karl rose and turned away from them. As he stared out towards the sea, Peter and Laura noticed the world around them wavering, as if it were starting to fall apart.

'I remember,' said Karl, he looked back at Risvu. 'My friend . . .'

'I hope this will not be the last time we meet, Prince.'

The great horse rose up on to its hind legs and disintegrated into a bright sparkling dust that gradually rose up to take its place among the stars.

Laura ran up to Karl, giggling, and put her hand on his shoulder. 'I would love to see the rest of the kingdom. We don't have to leave, just yet, your majesty.'

Peter then placed his hand on Karl's other shoulder. 'And I'm not sure if we even need this ship any more.'

Karl turned around and smiled as he saw Laura and Peter climb on to the side; they beckoned him to join them. Soon, all three of them were lined up balancing on the edge of the craft.

'Anything *is* possible!' laughed Karl Graham.

The night awaited the children with open arms as they leapt off, unafraid and arms outstretched, soaring out together into the unknown.

Angel Blood

Alyson Williams

My brother has eyes like chips of blue heaven. They twinkle like fairy lights when he is spinning his plates – flick and twist, flick and twist, spin-spin-spin like windmills on the wind. On and on, an island of dizzy waves clattering on our hallway floor. My brother is an angel, a guardian angel like the little gold pin that Grandma gave me for my birthday, its heart the blueness of my brother's eyes. We are twins, my brother and me, not identical twins, although my hair is as white as his. I have green eyes, like the moss in the garden or the floaty grass in the goldfish bowl. We grew together in our mother's womb, hugged together like rolled-up socks, being swished around in the sea inside Mummy, hidden under her heart.

My brother is called Autumn because he was born at the exact moment that Mummy saw a red leaf drift down into the October carpet of leaves outside the hospital window. I am called Kit after Grandad's Siamese cat who had eyes like mine; she died before we were born. I'm telling you this story while Autumn is spinning his plates on the garden path and watching the dust float up into the sunlight. He wants me to tell our story in my voice and my words, because Autumn doesn't talk in a way that many people can understand.

Autumn likes doing unusual things like this spinning of plates. Mummy says it's because he's autistic, but I think it's because he's an angel. He loves to watch the raindrops rolling down our window and will cry when it's summer and the clouds are dry. Sometimes, he will sit in the garden next to the birdbath and watch the sky for hours; I know he is looking for rain. Autumn's teacher, Mrs Bear, has made him a little book of pictures called 'symbols', which he can use to show us what he wants – it's like talking without a voice. Autumn has got a voice, a squeaky sort of peep-peep voice, not like mine, which is a proper talking one. He peep-peeps a lot when he is excited about his plates or when he's got a red balloon to blow raspberries on to.

Mrs Bear has made Autumn a symbol for rain on the weather page of his book and every day last summer he stuck it up on to his sticky board, so that the message said 'I want . . . RAIN'. When Mummy couldn't give it to him, he would go into the garden and sit by the birdbath and press his fingertips on to his eyelids so that he could see stars in his head. I know he was really sad. When the rain came at last, Autumn ran into the garden with just his socks on and was peep-peeping all over the place and licking the rain off the window. He looked really funny because he had one pink sock and one black-and-white striped sock on. He was very happy to see the rain – he told me with his heaven eyes and wispy angel voice in my head.

As well as the plates, red balloons and the rain, Autumn likes sticks. Long, short, lumpy, bumpy or plastic ones smooth as lollipops. I try to make railway tracks or Indian wigwams with the sticks but things like this make Autumn angry with me. When he's angry, his eyes look like thunderstorms and he talks in his digga-digga voice, low and deep like he's calling from inside a mountain. He doesn't like me touching his sticks; they are his special treasures. He lines them up in patterns – big to little, little to big, or arranged into long snakes around our bedroom. It can be difficult to walk around when he's had a snake day because if any of his snakes are moved, Autumn will scream and start slapping his legs. It makes me cry when he slaps himself so I never touch his snakes. He is my guardian angel and I try to be his, by protecting his snake sticks and praying for rain.

When we were tiny babies, Mummy said that she used to put us in the same cradle because I would cry when I was on my own. I have a picture in our bedroom of Autumn and me in the cradle. I've got a yellow hat like a dandelion and Autumn's is cherry red like his birthday leaf. In the picture, my arm is around Autumn's shoulder and his lips are pressed against my ear. My ears look like the dried-up apricots that Grandma brings for us. Sometimes, Autumn will look at the picture and bring it right up to his face as if he can look through it to remember our baby selves. When Autumn hits himself, this picture makes me cry because I want him to be quiet and safe with my arm wrapped around him.

You might be wondering why I'm telling you this story about Autumn and me. I've told you that he is my guardian angel and this is because Autumn saved my life. Today, it is summer again and we are in the garden watching the clouds and thinking about rain. I have been in the hospital for a long time and I love to sit here and feel the kissing breeze on my face and smell the sun baking in the stones. I have had leukaemia in my blood and it was very lonely in the hospital. I missed the peep-peep singing and whooshing of spinning plates. When Autumn came to see me, he just sat on the bed and stared at his fingers he was waggling in front of his eyes. He was frightened being on his own and Mummy said that he wouldn't eat much and was just sitting in the house, turning sticks over and over. I tried to tell him that he must eat his food so that he would be strong enough to spin plates but I think that he'd closed his ears. Autumn can do this like some people can close their eyes, it's like he's got little doors in his ears.

Mummy brought Autumn to see me every day but he didn't seem to be feeling any happier. Grandad asked the doctor if Autumn could stay in the hospital with me, but the doctor didn't think this was a good idea because of germs. Mummy told the doctor about Autumn being my angel and about our dandelion and cherry picture. The doctor said that he could understand about that type of love but still 'rules were there for a reason' and he 'couldn't take the chance'. After this, Mummy didn't bring Autumn any more because he would get too upset and slap himself when he had to leave me. When I didn't see Autumn every day, my blood started to get more poorly, and I could tell that everyone thought I was going to die. Thinking about dying made me very frightened, because if I died then Autumn would be on his own and no one would understand about the rain and the red balloons and the sticks. Angels don't talk to many people and my brother needs people to know about all his special things. He needs people who can talk without words.

Through my window in the hospital, I could see a big tree holding out his arms like Autumn does when the rain comes. It stood still in the sun, but danced and dipped when the wind blew; sometimes it looked like a wild monster with a million ponytails. On the day the doctor came with Mummy, the tree was still and waiting; it was like someone had turned the sound off or its batteries were dead. The doctor said that there was nothing else they could do to make me better and that I needed something called a 'bone marrow transplant'. He said that because I was a twin, Autumn would be the best person to do this. His blood would match mine and they could just pour some of his blood into me. He said that everyone thought that Autumn would be very frightened if he had to do this – he wouldn't understand because of the autism. I told them that Autumn understood with his heart and not with words, and this was why he could talk to clouds. I told them that to tell Autumn something really important you had to talk to yourself in your heart until the most important words in the message were clear. Then you had to sit with Autumn and spin plates, until he knew that you were waiting for him to listen – like waiting for someone to answer the telephone. When he felt sure you were waiting, quietly, calmly, then Autumn would open the doors in his ears and you could give him the heart words. The doctor thought this sounded a bit too complicated and I could tell that he didn't know much about talking to angels. Mummy said that she could talk to Autumn if the doctor would change his rules so that we could be together in the hospital.

So that is what happened.

Mrs Bear made some new symbols for Autumn's book, which told different stories about hospitals and blood, and Autumn had a bed next to mine in a special little room where there were no germs. He brought lots of sticks with him, which had to be cleaned in the special cleaning machine to take all the bugs out of them. Mr Stone, the cleaning man said that he'd never had to do sticks before and that Autumn must be an 'unusual chap'. I told him about angels and he said that he thought I was probably right; there are lots of angels in the world but people generally haven't got the right type of eyes to see them.

There were lots of tests and needles and Autumn cried in his digga-digga voice, but this time it was a small, sad noise instead of a mountain angry type. I told him that he was doing good and stuck a smiley symbol on his sticky board to show I was happy with him. I helped him to blow up the red balloons he was getting because of his being so brave; there were so many of them it was like being in the middle of a raspberry. A lady working in the kitchen had sent him some plates that couldn't break, for when he felt like spinning.

The doctor without angel-seeing eyes could see that there was a lot of happiness in our room and I think he was glad that he broke the rules about the germs. Mummy had brought us a calendar to show Autumn how many more days were left before we could go home and this helped him to feel happier. I was a bit frightened about the operation, but I knew that Autumn would help me to feel OK about it all, when the time came. Mummy told us that she was very proud of how we helped each other and that we were special brothers.

On our operation day, Grandma brought us new pyjamas – dandelion yellow for me and cherry red for Autumn – and we sat in our beds like two of Grandma's hard-boiled sweets that she brings us after school. Autumn had built snake sticks all over his bed sheet and had balloons tied to his slippers, where his pink sock and black- and-white striped sock were poking out. Some of the nurses thought this was funny but I knew that Autumn was building a home for himself in this strange place and this would keep him safe in his heart until Mummy could take us away to our real home.

Grandad took a picture of us that day and now it's on the wall in our bedroom, next to the cradle picture, so that I can see it every day and remember to be brave like Autumn. Some people think you have to be very old, or very rich, or very clever, to be brave but I know that Autumn is the bravest person there is. So this is why he is my guardian angel – he brought his precious sticks to a strange place and let the doctors give me some of his blood when mine was broken. I have angel blood inside me now and its magic will keep me spinning and dancing for ever.

Message From Mel

Viv Seaman

My mum's great, but a lousy cook. Before she knew Mrs Robertson, meal-times were disaster areas. Huge bullets of burnt junk food would stare up at me.

'Mel, I've spent hours over a hot stove. Eat it!'

Mum is inclined to exaggerate. Her voice would get faster and higher.

'Melanie, starving children would love that dinner.'

'Then pack it up and post it to them!' I'd scream. 'They're welcome to it.' My teeth'd clamp together, so none of the muck could be forced in.

My mum's clever (she's got a really important job), so you'd think she'd have taken the hint from the telly about burgers and mad cows and things. If it wasn't enough to feed us on nothing but junk food, she was always burning it. Even the fish fingers were singed and the crinkle-cut chips so scorched their edges burnt straight.

I suppose it's the luck of the draw which grown-ups you end up with as your family. George Robertson next door has got a great cook for a mother. She never uses junk food. Makes bread, uses loads of fresh vegetables. . . She's really good at the health bit. And George? Does he know how lucky he is? 'Course not. He's always sneaking in here and ogling Mum's cooking, fish fingers or microwave dinners or whatever, until she invites him to stay and share ours. Or he used to, until *it* happened.

It might have been a rotten day for everyone else, but for me it was brilliant. Because of *it,* Mum and George's mum met. We hadn't lived in our house very long – there was just me and Mum now, so she had to go back to work. Pick up her career she called it. I started a new primary school and got to know lots of people but Mum, being out at work, didn't know anyone that much. She didn't have time for friends, she said.

On the day *it* happened, me and Stacey and Zak and Sam hung around at the end of the playground poking our legs through the fence and writing our names in the mud with our feet. It wasn't a proper fence, just a builder's thing to keep us off the works.

The works was the site where they were building a swimming pool for our school. Now it was ready and we were going to have a grand opening ceremony. The head had been going on about it for months.

'I shall expect the very best behaviour.' Miss Pinkerton practised the same speech in assembly all week. You could see she meant it.

'The board of governors and a reporter from the local paper will be present, also the school inspector. It is important we are seen at our very best.'

On the day, I felt quite guilty about it as I had forgotten to remind Mum, so I wasn't wearing a clean dress. It didn't matter as Mum wouldn't know until it was too late. And I am not that mucky. I can wear a dress for three days and you wouldn't know. Unlike George, always getting into messy places, doing stupid experiments, or mucking around with that dog of his, Scratch. Mum and I saw him on the building site covered in mud the night before *it* happened, crawling all over the cover the builders had put on the pool, lying down on top of it, playing with Scratch.

On the afternoon of the grand opening, loads of parents arrived. The whole school was sitting cross-legged in rows by the pool. Miss Pinkerton, wearing her 'especially for visitors grin', led the important people up the wobbly, makeshift steps of the specially built platform. She started introducing them in her slime-ball voice.

'Our dear lady mayor, the chairman of governors, councillor Hodgekiss, councillor Mrs Beamish and our school inspector, Mr Hill.' She droned on and on. Most of us had switched off by then. It was pretty gross sitting there on damp grass with our bottoms going numb. Better than maths, though.

They were an odd bunch, all dressed in grey and looking miserable. There were nine of them. Hodgekiss looked grumpy, his mouth hidden under a chinese mandarin moustache. Mrs Beamish had this stupid grin and all her bits wobbled out of time with each other when she sat down. She smothered the chair. While the speeches were on, I just watched her wobble.

'And finally,' the lady mayor was finishing her speech, 'I declare this swimming pool well and truly open.'

The caretaker began winding the handle to pull back the cover and everyone gasped. Everything went spookily silent for a minute.

'Arrgh!'

'Oh . . . oh, what's happened?'

'Good Heavens. It's bright red water.'

'Sabotage.'

'Can't they get anything right?'

Grown-ups were yelling all over the place. Everything went mad. What we could all see was ghastly red water in the pool. All us kids were on our feet, screaming and crying, pushing nearer and nearer the edge. The din was horrific. The inspector was furiously scribbling notes. Councillor Hodgekiss mopped his forehead. Someone said he had drunk too much of Miss Pinkerton's wine at lunch-time. He kept muttering, 'Never again, never again.'

Mrs Beamish, frozen with fear, wobbled like a porpoise on her chair, then, catching sight of a line of polystyrene floats at the far end of the pool, mistook them for a body.

'It's a corpse, a dead body. Help! Murder!' she

screamed and people gasped and whispers of 'blood', 'murder', whisked all round the pool, getting louder and louder. Up on the platform, all nine guests were leaping about, more scared than us kids. Then *it* happened.

There was a crack. Then another one, ear-splittingly loud. You could almost feel the platform straining under the weight. Then the platform's front supports gave up and crashed into the pool. The platform tipped forwards at a steep angle and all the visitors catapulted, one after another, into the revolting red water.

It was better than telly. Mrs Beamish landed in the depths below with an incredible belly-flop and caused a tidal wave, drenching Years one and two. All the teachers panicked like mad, screaming and slithering in the wet and trying to save the little kids from slipping into the pool.

All the grey-suited visitors flapped about in red water, like a school of soggy whales. Mrs Beamish kept disappearing under the surface then popping up again, spouting a puce water jet, before hauling herself up on the lady mayor's heavy gold chain and dragging her under.

My gran says we need a bit more colour in our lives. We certainly had that.

'George Robertson, come here at once!' Miss Pinkerton screamed over the P.A. system. I should have guessed. We had seen him, Mum and I, playing there the day before. Come to think of it, his fingers had looked all red in the playground that morning. He was always up to something.

The newspaper reporter had a field day. According to him, George had been experimenting after watching a programme on TV about colouring sausages bright red and green and blue to see if children found them more appetizing. George's mum had been dyeing natural wool (she's into all that kind of stuff) and he had got hold of a load of her dye.

Anyway, George was nearly suspended. Our school's street cred went right up with the posh pupils at St Andrew's up the road, but not with the parents. Mrs Beamish was never normal again. Miss Pinkerton seemed to lose all her go after that, once she had screamed blue murder at George. All her get up and go, got up and went.

The school's big day fizzled out. Well, it was washed out I suppose. As most of the parents were there, Miss Pinkerton told everyone they could go home early. Trouble was, Mum wasn't due to collect me for another hour. George's mum was worried about me, which was really kind of her. It's not very nice when everyone knows your son has done something that bad.

She took me home to her house and phoned Mum at work to let her know I was OK. And that's how Mum's cooking got better.

Mum came to collect me and stopped for a cup of tea and a quick chat, which lasted over an hour and turned into a recipe-swapping session. I don't think Mrs Robertson was all that impressed with Wong's Chinese Take-away menu that Mum showed her, but Mum got some great ideas and started trying them out.

I went into Year six the next term and George went to secondary school, where he did proper experiments. I've got to admit, it was quite good going to a school that he made famous.

Whatever they say about George, my digestive system was well pleased.

Photographic Memory

Joanna Wilson

'Get out from under my feet, Robert. I've got enough to do this afternoon without you being a nuisance. Go upstairs and play. You've plenty of toys. I don't want to see you for the rest of the afternoon!'

Robert walked upstairs. He hated Sundays. Especially Sunday afternoons. The countdown to another week of school and another week of imprisonment in a hot, sticky classroom.

Robert's heart sank as he went into his room and saw all the toys he had out on the floor. Toy soldiers standing on guard. Red Indians collapsed after battle. He wasn't in the mood for tidying his toys away – it somehow gestured that he was prepared to give up on the weekend before it was truly over. He wasn't in the mood to sit in an untidy room, either. He walked out on to the landing and tiptoed across the floor into his parents' room. The open window aired the room with a fresh breeze of newly cut grass. Summer was here.

On his parents' bed sat the family photo album, bursting with pictures that illustrated Robert's family's life. It was an old leather album, blue in colour but fading from years of use. He opened it; the first photo to catch his eye was of his parents when they were at university together. He'd seen these photos time and time again; his mum was always showing them to anyone that came to the house.

He turned the page and saw the professional photos of his parents' wedding. His mum looked young and beautiful under the layers of white lace. His dad looked like he did when Arsenal had won the FA Cup - happy and joyful, like he himself had shot the winning goal. On the ground was a coloured speck. Tiny, but visible. Robert looked closer, peering into the picture, trying to focus on the small flecks of colour. It looked like a butterfly – perhaps it was confetti. He looked closer. And closer, staring and focusing, squinting and peering; trying to make sense of what he saw. His eyes ached and through the pain of this he noticed something very odd about the photo in front of him. For the photo was no longer just a two-dimensional image lying in the album. It moved. It played out before him like a cinema film. His parents were walking, the confetti was falling and the congregation were smiling and laughing. He could see everything, as it must have been that day. Saw it all playing out before him like he was just another invited guest, watching the day go by. His mother's dress rustled in the breeze and the trees swayed in the background as if celebrating the wedding vows that had just been made.

The photo was alive. It breathed with energy and life.

It was just as if Robert was reminiscing about a day in his past. One that was remembered in vivid detail and vibrant colour. But Robert was not even born when this photo had been taken. He was not tangled up in his memory – he was looking at a picture that had come to life, even though real-life had moved on by a decade now.

Robert blinked, unable to sustain this constant peering. The picture snapped back to being the photograph it always had been. Stiff and posed like the toy soldiers in his room. There was no movement, his parents had returned to statues again. Robert gasped in wonder. What had just happened? Had he been dreaming?

His first instinct was to run downstairs to tell his mother. Tell her what he had seen, let her see for herself what was hidden in the old photo album that usually sat collecting dust on the unsteady bookcase. Then he stopped himself. This was his secret. This was his miracle. Besides, she had told him that she didn't want to see him for the rest of the afternoon. He turned the page and decided to venture deeper into the album's collection of memories. . .

He moved on a few pages until he came to a photo of himself when he was about seven. His brown hair was tousled and uncut, his eyes shimmering in the summer sun. It was taken two years ago, on holiday in Cornwall. He was holding a rock-pool net, meant for catching tiny fish but he had never managed to even catch seaweed in its weaved web. Again he looked closer. He stared and he focused, he squinted and he peered. . .

A familiar world came to life. He saw his eyes darting around the rock-pool, searching for a flicker of life in the water. He noticed how he gingerly negotiated his way around the sides of the water, careful not to slide on the slippery rocks and mindful not to catch his toes on the sharp mussels that rested there. People were building fortresses from soggy sand, children squealing as they failed to jump the waves successfully. It was like another world. One he knew and remembered, but one that he thought had been put to the back of his memory.

He looked away, eager to move on to another photo and another world that he could escape to. He quickly turned the pages, searching for a photograph that caught his imagination. As he neared the back of the album, the photos became far more recent. These were photos that must have been taken in the last few weeks. Polaroid snaps of him on his bike, playing in the street. He'd not been aware that while he was cycling back and forth on the pavement, his parents had been recording fragments of his life. Snapshots of his existence.

Robert was not interested in entering into these photos, though. It was his life and he lived in it every day. He wanted to escape to another world, where he didn't know the faces and didn't know the surroundings. He decided to flick back through the book, right to the beginning, where the pictures showed a black and white world, before colour photography had been invented.

A small, crinkled photo caught his eye. A young man, in an army uniform, smiling broadly at the camera. His great-grandad. A man he had never known. He had died in battle in 1944, shortly after this photo had been taken. Robert smiled back at him. This was the photo he wanted to go into. This was the world he wanted to be a part of.

He looked at the photograph, staring and focused, squinting and peering. His own world swam away behind him and the new world enveloped him. The first thing Robert noticed was the noise. So much noise. So many people shouting and chattering in anticipation of receiving their post from home. His great-grandad was in the crowd waiting patiently. Listening intently for any mention of his name being called.

'Charlie Banks.'

His great-grandfather ran forward. His smile wide and his hand reaching forward for the small envelope. He broke away from the crowd and searched for a quiet place where he could sit down and relish every word from his loved ones at home. He sat down on a grassy bank and opened the envelope, taking care not to tear any of its contents. Who was it from? Robert wondered. What were the words his great-grandfather had yet to read? Was it from his wife telling him about the birth of their new baby?

There were so many men rushing to find spaces of their own now, tiny plots of silence and tranquillity, so they could be alone and undisturbed. These letters were their only link to the outside world, away from the war and away from conflict. They treasured such moments of peace.

Robert looked back towards his great-grandfather. He was absorbed in the letter and Robert could just see tears forming in his eyes. A man who was so brave in battle, coping through fear and the death of his comrades, but it was words from home that could melt his heart. Robert looked closer, seeing tears were now streaming down his cheeks. Robert desperately wanted to reach out and be of comfort to him – a link to his family life and the world he had been ordered to leave behind. He tried to reach forward but he realised that this was not the way it worked. He could see this new world move in front of him, and watch it like it had been all that time ago, but he couldn't be a part of that time because he wasn't yet born. He had his seat in the cinema but he wasn't allowed to move seats when the lights went down.

His great-grandfather's tears smothered his face. Robert's heart went out to him. Then a delighted grin spread across his great-grandfather's face. Robert smiled too, realising that these were not tears of sorrow, but tears of joy.

'ENEMY ATTACK!'

Robert's heart leapt. A soldier ran past yelling the warning, gun already to fire, adrenaline pumping. The tears were brushed away and his great-grandfather's face changed to show determination and strength. All thoughts of home were,put to the back of his mind, saved for later when he had a quiet moment to himself.

'Robert, your dinner's ready. I won't call you again,' came an external voice. His mother. His own world. He snapped out of the photo and blinked hard, trying to compose himself, readjust to his old surroundings.

'I'm coming,' he called back, playing for time. Time to think about all he'd just seen. But his mother was already walking into the room. He snapped the album shut.

'What have you been up to, darling? I've been calling you for ages. Didn't you hear me?'

'I've just been tidying up my room. Thought it was a bit messy.'

'That makes a change! Come on, dinner's ready. It'll be getting cold'.

They walked down the stairs together. His heart pounding, desperate to be alone with the album again. His mother looked at him quizzically.

'What's that you've got in your hand?'

Robert looked down. It was a piece of paper. Discoloured with age. It was a letter.

'I found it in the family album,' he replied. It wasn't entirely the truth, but it would do. For now.

The Piano Player's Hands

Cynan Jones

The Piano Player was asleep when his hands woke up and began to argue.

That day he had given a terrific concert, his best ever, everybody said. People had clapped and clapped while he waved his right hand to the crowd with pride, his left hand casually in his pocket out of sight, or mopping the sweat from his brow with a silk hanky.

During the night, while the Piano Player snored like someone playing a tuba in the bath, his hands started to talk.

'Thank you for supporting me today,' said the Right Hand, tired after his dazzling performance.

The Left Hand was angry.

'Oh!' he said, sarcastically. 'My pleasure.'

'What's the matter?' asked the Right Hand.

'You're always the star,' said the Left. 'You always get the beautiful tunes. I've heard people whistling them after our concerts, walking away from the hall. Nobody notices the work I have to do, down there, below you . . . plod, plod. . .'

It was not the first time they had argued.

'At least you don't always *have* to entertain people,' said the Right Hand. 'It's tiring. And sometimes I get bored of playing the same things, the same few tunes over and over during a piece, so people *can* remember them, and whistle them to themselves. You can change everything depending on what you play – while I'm just there for decoration.'

'But you get the applause.'

'Only because I am more obvious.'

'I want applause. I want people to notice me. And it's not just in concerts, either. It's in everything. You're his favourite.'

'What do you mean?' asked the Right Hand.

'He waves you to the crowd.'

'And you wipe the sweat from his brow.'

'You hold his glasses of champagne when he stands in parties.'

'And you scratch an itch, or brush away a fly.'

'You shake the hands of the politicians he meets, and the princes and important people.'

'And you hold his child when he walks in the park.'

Sometimes, the Right Hand envied the Left. It was true he was more dazzling – had more attention in crowds, or was called upon for grand gestures; but he sometimes wished for the simple tasks. Things which to him seemed more important, that happened to keep a man comfortable.

'You keep his wedding ring safe, and wear his watch,'

said the Right Hand.

'I have to pick his nose!' argued the Left. 'And I smack his child when he misbehaves in the park.'

The Left Hand found it difficult to understand why the Right Hand felt so sorry for himself.

The Right Hand loved the fact that the Left was more free to change; because nobody watched him as much, and they did not really expect things from him. For half a song he might plod, plod, repeating the same line underneath a high tune, but then, when people had almost forgotten him, when he had become more part of the piano than part of the music, he would change gently, and make everything different. And people would be moved, surprised, lulled as they were, expecting nothing, concentrating only on the obvious.

'Maybe we should swap,' said the Left Hand. And they agreed.

And so it was that one day, on the morning of a big concert, the Piano Player woke up and found himself in terrible trouble. He tried to clean his teeth but his hands just would not work. They simply refused. Trying to tie his shoelaces was a disaster. And so was trying to eat his egg for breakfast. He spent the whole day tripping over and hungry!

By the time the Piano Player arrived at the concert hall, he was a nervous wreck. He even had to ask a viola player to tie his bow-tie for him, which took quite some time! 'It will be OK for the concert,' he kept saying to himself, 'it will be OK . . .'

But it wasn't OK. The concert was a disaster.

The Right Hand smiled as he played beautiful chords, and arpeggios, and counter melodies, little snatches of the tune, louder or quieter, loving the way he changed the music. The Left Hand thundered around the bass notes, banging out the famous tunes too low for people to whistle, or trilling and turning round special notes, proud that he could show the audience that he too could dance. But it sounded like a lorry reversing. The Piano Player was distraught.

When the concert finished, nobody clapped. Some of them put one hand or the other to their mouth to whistle rudely, or threw their programmes to the stage in disgust. Nobody put their hands together to show appreciation – to show their happiness as they usually did. And the Piano Player's hands felt very, very selfish.

They knew then that they were one as important as the other. That they were not the same, and couldn't do the other's work. They realised that they were made different so that they could support one another, to create something complete. And so, they didn't fight any more. From that day on, each hand concentrated only on what made it special, and didn't try to be something it was not. And the next concert was the greatest ever heard.

Un-bearable Behaviour

Oliver Davies

Now once upon a time, in a house in a forest, there lived three bears.

Wait, I hear you cry, not this old turnip! I've heard this story a million times before, why should I be bothered to sit down and read it again?

Well, you may think that you've heard this story before but I can assure you that you've never heard the full story. Today, we are going to be looking for the truth behind Goldilocks and the three bears – and nothing but the truth.

So, let me begin again. Once upon a time, in a house in a forest, there lived three bears. There was a Daddy bear, a Mummy bear and a Baby bear. Now, at this point, I really should point out that bears are not entirely suited to living in houses. Indeed, most bears have accepted this to be a fact; which is why you will find the majority of bears living in caves or other such places. Most reasonable bears would accept that they are not fully equipped to deal with a house and the appliances within.

But not these bears. You see, these bears had the

impression that it was natural for bears to live in a house. A life of foraging for food and snaring wild salmon from streams was not for them; instead they preferred to sit around a table and eat porridge. And not even porridge with honey – which would at least be more understandable for a bear.

Our story begins one morning when Mummy bear, having done her best to cope with the disadvantage of furry paws, cooked a saucepan full of boiling hot porridge. We have no true record of the conversation that went on inside the house that day, but we can hazard a guess that it went something like this. The bears, sat waiting for their porridge, realised that their breakfast was likely to be too hot to consume. It is well known that bears have an aversion to scalding their tongues and so, one of the bears – we believe it to be Daddy bear – suggested that all three of the bears should go out for a walk.

'If we go for a walk, the porridge will have cooled down by the time we return.'

The bears accepted that the porridge was too hot – this is important and we shall return to it later. They dressed themselves in coats, hats, boots and mittens (again, an act that is quite un-bear like) and set out for a walk in the woods. They shut the door behind them but did not lock it.

Now, no more than two minutes after the bears had departed their house, a little girl called Goldilocks came skipping down the forest path. Goldilocks was a good girl (with excellent character references) who came from a good family and had never been in trouble with the law previously.

She noticed the bears' house and she noticed that the door was open. Not just unlocked, but open – gaping ajar so that Goldilocks was able to see all the way into the bears' dining-room. At this point, Goldilocks' neighbourly instincts set in. Seeing an open door, she couldn't help but investigate. Why, perhaps a little old lady was trapped inside a wardrobe with a wolf in her bed – Goldilocks had heard about these sorts of things on the news, and so showed immense bravery by stepping past the heavy wooden door and over the threshold. Bravery which, I believe, should be commended.

Well, having stepped inside the bears' house, Goldilocks called out.

'Hello? Is there anybody there?'

The house was silent.

Creeping further inside, Goldilocks noticed the dining-room table for the first time and the three bowls of porridge lined up across the tabletop. She'd walked a long way through the forest and, being a little girl, was extremely hungry. We must, therefore, excuse her behaviour in trying the food laid out before her.

Picking up a spoon from the side, she took a large scoop from the biggest bowl at the head of the table (this was the bowl belonging to Daddy bear but, at this point, Goldilocks was not to know this). She took a mouthful of porridge and discovered, to her horror, that it was burning hot. Goldilocks spat the porridge out, but the damage had been done and she had suffered a number of painful blisters to her delicate mouth.

Let me remind you again. The bears *knew* the porridge was too hot, which was why they went for a walk in the forest. They knew it could scald but, nevertheless, they left the door open and placed no warning about the likely heat of the porridge – clearly an act of criminal negligence on their part.

Now, at this point, Goldilocks was dazed and confused. Who can say what mental state she would have been in when in such excruciating pain. All we know is that, in this disturbed state of mind, Goldilocks tried Mummy bear's porridge and ate the entire bowl of porridge that had been set aside for Baby bear. Perhaps this was a desperate attempt to ease the agony of her inflamed mouth. We may never know, but it has resulted in Goldilocks developing a profound phobia about porridge.

Nevertheless, after this distressing incident, Goldilocks felt the need to sit down and so entered the sitting-room.

First of all, she tried Daddy bear's chair, but she found that the cushion was much too hard and uncomfortable. Next, she tried Mummy bear's chair, but found that was the exact opposite – a squidgy, voluminous cushion that sucked her down like quicksand. Finally, her eyes settled on Baby bear's chair.

Now, some history about Baby bear's chair. It had been constructed by Daddy bear and, as I'm sure you'll appreciate, a bear is hindered by his claws when trying to use a hammer and nails. I'm sure he did his best but, quite frankly, his best just wasn't good enough.

So Goldilocks, spying this chair that appeared to be just the right size and looked extremely comfortable, sat down. There was a moment where everything seemed all right, then suddenly, without warning, the wooden chair splintered and fell to pieces, sending Goldilocks sprawling to the hard stone floor where she landed most awkwardly. Independent medical experts have said she was extremely lucky not to incur a permanent back injury and Goldilocks herself has voiced fears that she may never be able to play netball again because of the muscle damage.

And so, a girl's life is damaged by a poorly constructed chair – a chair that any reasonable bear would not even have considered trying to construct.

However, Goldilocks, being a plucky sort of girl, recovered as best she could but – possibly due to some form of concussion sustained in the fall – felt the urgent desire to sleep and so began exploring the upstairs of the house.

She found a room containing three beds and from the

clothing and items beside each bed, decided that the first belonged to Daddy bear, the second to Mummy bear and the third to Baby bear.

Of course, being tired, she immediately tried the first bed she came to but found that the mattress on Daddy bear's bed was far too hard, its springs digging painfully into her already bruised back. In her confused state, she regrets that she did get into the bed still wearing her muddy shoes, but this is not something which she should be judged upon.

Next she tried Mummy bear's bed but, here, she found that the mattress was much too soft for a little girl and so she turned finally to Baby bear's bed.

The smallest of the three beds, Baby bear's bed was the perfect size for Goldilocks and, as soon as she slipped between the sheets, she realised that it was also perfectly comfortable. Before her head had even touched the pillow, Goldilocks had fallen into a deep and peaceful sleep.

It was at this moment that the bears chose to return from their walk in the woods. They ambled their way into the dining-room and quickly spotted the half-eaten porridge. Each bear noticed that some of their porridge was missing; with Baby bear pointing out that his had been eaten all up.

Next, the bears moved to the sitting- room, where they realised that someone had been sitting in their chairs. Noticing the broken wood on the floor, the bears realised that Baby bear's chair had been broken but, rather than being concerned as to the health of the person who had suffered at the hands of his poor carpentry, Daddy bear at this point grew angry.

We believe the bears stormed upstairs to the bedroom, examining the three beds in turn. Daddy bear noted the disturbed sheets on his bed. Mummy bear noticed the muddy footprints in her bed, but Baby bear noticed that someone was still asleep in his bed. The three bears moved across the room to have a look.

Goldilocks awoke to the sound of growling and found she was looking up at three wild-looking bears. Their teeth were bared, their eyes glinted evily and their claws looked sharp enough to rip a little girl into a hundred pieces. It was a purely natural reaction that she should scream loudly and dive through the nearest window. I think any one of us would have done the same thing if confronted with that appalling sight.

Goldilocks was quite fortunate to land amongst a bed of shrubs for they broke her fall and meant she only sustained minor ankle injuries (which, nonetheless, have since held back her physical development) rather than more serious – potentially fatal ones. In this pitiful state, poor Goldilocks managed to limp home through the forest.

Now, the three bears have since argued that Goldilocks committed an offence of breaking and entering by going into their house, that she stole their porridge and that she caused criminal damage by breaking their chairs and damaging their bed linen. In short, they have tried to make this whole incident look like Goldilocks' fault, which is complete nonsense.

Goldilocks was the victim in all of this. She entered a house through an already open door in an attempt to be a good citizen. Through criminal negligence, she was scalded by boiling porridge and has since suffered a phobia about porridge. Through negligent craftsmanship, she suffered a grievous back injury when the chair she sat on fell apart. And then, as a final straw, she was confronted by three fierce and vicious bears and had to flee for her life through a first floor window.

Since all of this, Goldilocks has suffered a deep fear of bears – indeed, she cannot stand the sight of even the smallest of teddy bears for fear that it might attack her. A young life has been permanently damaged by a series of wilful and negligent acts by a family of bears who have refused to accept the limitations of their species.

That is the truth, the whole truth and nothing but the truth. And it was on that evidence that I managed to secure Goldilocks an out-of-court settlement for £60,000 against the three bears. Hopefully, that money will help her rebuild her shattered life.

Now, must dash, I've got a Big Bad Wolf sitting in my office with an excellent case of post-traumatic stress against three little pigs . . .

Kidnap on the Cut

Val Williamson

I was just about to scramble up on to the smelly wreck of a narrowboat. 'Ow!' something hard and sharp hit the back of my neck. I heard a pebble clatter behind me. 'That hurt!' I turned, but there was nobody there.

Dad's friend Mike had found this old sunken narrowboat and wanted Dad to help restore it.

'This is a real piece of history, right on our own doorstep,' said Dad, who was crazy about canals. 'It'll be a privilege to work on her!'

Mike had already organised hoisting the boat out of the water and shoring it up so high I could walk underneath it. He had arranged to use part of the old wharf buildings as store-sheds, too. Now, he needed craftsmen like Dad to help take the boat apart and rebuild it.

Mike and Dad examined the hulk, going on about *clinkers* and *carvels* and other things I'd never heard of. They seemed to have forgotten me altogether. I eyed the cabin end of the boat again, desperate to get up there and take a look.

The one thing I did know about narrowboats was that the insides of the cabins were usually painted with pictures of castles. I had hoped that Dad would take me for a day out to visit the Boat Museum that summer, perhaps even to have a ride in a narrowboat, but he'd never have the time now.

I had just worked out how to scramble up to the cabin when a boy materialised.

'Don't touch it!' he said, 'it's dangerous.'

'What would you know?'

He looked strange, with his ragged-edged trousers and thick tweedy wool jacket, and a pair of boots that he might have borrowed from a tramp. 'Don't you know it's summer?'

'I know plenty.' He straightened himself up and balled his fists, preparing for a fight. 'Them planks is rotten, anybody can see that.'

I remembered hearing Mike say that the cabin was the rottenest part of the boat. Something to do with poking up above the mud in drought years.

'It looks safe enough to me,' I said. Who did he think he was, appearing out of nowhere, telling me what to do?

'There's nowt safe about boats,' he said gloomily, 'you be careful.'

Just then, Dad called that it was time to go home. I turned to look back as we walked the blue pebble path that led along the wharf, but the boy had disappeared.

By the time I had broken up from school, Dad and Mike were all set to get started.

'You can be mate, Nick,' Dad said, 'there'll be plenty of fetching and carrying for you to do.'

Their first job was to carefully strip away rotten wood from the hull. I was to stand by with a wheelbarrow to cart away the bits, and stack them in the far warehouse.

There seemed to be more standing than carting, though. They tried to make it interesting for me by telling me stories about the old horse-drawn narrowboats. They told me some traditional canal ghost stories, too, but I didn't believe in ghosts.

I soon got bored with the lack of action. I had noticed some doors to other rooms inside the sheds, so next time I emptied the wheelbarrow I decided to go exploring.

'Phaw, it's very dark and dusty in here! Horrible!' Your own voice sounds quite friendly when you're alone in a spooky place.

I opened the door in the back wall and saw wooden stairs with a rope handhold leading down.

'Aat-shoo!'

'Who's that?'

A sharp stone stung the back of my head.

'Ouch!'

The boy was behind me, a catapult in his hand.

'You be more careful,' he said.

'What's it to you?' I grumbled, but I was disappointed that we were once again arguing. I needed a friend and he was just about the right age, even if he did speak with a funny accent and dress like a character from a history book.

'Them old ropes is rotten,' he said, 'always was. It's the damp.'

'Yeah? So, how come you managed to find that out and lived to tell the tale?'

He didn't say anything, just looked at me oddly.

'Nick?' It was Dad. Mike was with him.

'What's that door doing open?' Mike asked, 'it's not safe down there.'

'I know,' I muttered, looking round, but the boy had disappeared again.

It wasn't until I was lying in bed that night that I remembered that the sneeze I had heard had come from down those steps, and not from behind me.

But if not that boy, then who? I wondered.

A strange little thought popped into my head for a second. 'Nah! I don't believe in ghosts!'

Every day after that, from the minute our van turned on to the wasteland behind the sheds, I would be on the lookout, but there was never a sign of the boy again.

'Remember, you're never to go exploring in there again,' Dad said, 'old buildings are dangerous.'

I started taking a football with me, to while away the boring bits when Dad and Mike got into a huddle about the next phase of the work, or went off to buy more materials. I was alone on the wasteland when the combination of a strong kick and a gust of wind walloped the ball towards the canal.

'Oh, no!'

I was chasing under the boat towards the stretch of blue pebbles when the boy suddenly appeared right in front of me. I dug my heels in, skidded and sprawled on my back with my feet overhanging the water.

'I told you be careful!' he said, grinning at me.

'Charming,' I scrambled to my feet. 'Oh, look at my football!'

It had floated right out into the middle of the canal.

'That could have been you,' he commented.

He was right, I had been running so fast I could never have stopped if he hadn't bobbed up in front of me at the crucial moment. As usual, he had turned up when I was in danger.

'Yes,' I said, suddenly shivery, 'thanks. What's your name?'

'It's Josh. You're on your own,' he said, that morose look on his face. He took the catapult from his pocket, replaced it with a few of the roundest blue pebbles from the path, and started making target practice against the wall. 'You shouldn't be on the towpath on your own, anything could happen.'

'Oh yeah, like what?'

'You could get taken.'

'Taken? What do you mean, "taken"?'

'Boys gets taken.'

'Dad wouldn't have left me alone if it was that dangerous,' I said, but the shivers wouldn't stop. 'There's nobody here but you and me.'

Josh gave me that odd look again. 'What about him over in the sheds?'

The shivers walked even more coldly down my spine. 'The sheds? Who's in the sheds?'

'There's a man over there.'

I remembered the ghostly sneeze.

'He's up to no good I reckon, skulking about at night and hiding stuff.'

That didn't sound very ghostly. 'Hiding stuff? What stuff?'

'I don't know,' Josh said.

'Show me,' I said.

'No, you're not to go there, I heard your dad say.'

'Well, my dad's not here now.'

'Your dad's good to you. My dad was good to us, but you can't sleep ten children in a narrowboat cabin.'

'You lived on a narrowboat?'

'You wouldn't like it,' he said, 'too much like hard work for you!'

I was remembering something Mike had been saying just the other day.

Mike had told me how the old boatmen had used a catapult to aim a pebble at the horse's backside, to spur it into action if it had stopped moving.

'Is that why you had a catapult?'

Josh didn't reply, but instead asked, 'When are they going to start on the cabin?'

'I don't know. Last, probably. Got to get the hull right first.'

'Wish they'd hurry up,' Josh said, 'I hate that cabin.'

'You've been in there?'

Our van came crunching across the wasteland. While I was waving to Dad, Josh vanished. I was a bit annoyed when he didn't reappear again that day, because I wanted to ask him to make me a catapult of my own.

The next weekend, there were a lot of volunteers to help with the boat. A woman from the Boat Museum had decided that the cabin would have to be taken apart bit by bit, and the painted panels preserved. I was desperate to see inside, but they made me keep away.

I wandered off, fingering a length of elastic in my pocket, looking for a shaped bit of wood to help make it into a catapult.

There was a man hovering about in the shadows, but he didn't seem too interested in the boat. It was very dark and shadowy along there, a bit spooky really, with the roof of the warehouse overhanging and blocking out the light.

Half way along, I realised the man was following me. If I stopped, he stopped. When I started off, he started off. The hairs on the back of my neck prickled. What was he up to?

I was too far from the boat to call for help, so I started to run, but caught my foot on something and went sprawling. The man was beside me as I stood up, clamping his hand over my mouth and dragging me into a dark doorway.

Josh appeared. 'Leave 'im alone!' he said.

The man stopped. 'What're you going to do about it?'

'Leave 'im alone!' Josh stepped nearer, pulling the catapult from his pocket.

The blue pebble must have hurt, shot at such close range. The man let go of me and staggered back a step or two.

'I'll get you for that!' he rumbled.

But Josh had already set another pebble flying. It caught the man in the middle of his forehead. He staggered backwards again, right into the canal.

'Come on,' Josh said, grabbibg hold of me and running towards the boat, where everybody was standing around chatting.

I found Dad and poured out my story about the man.

'As it happens,' he said, 'the police are already on their way.'

'What? But how did they know?' I asked, but no one answered; everybody was running around trying to catch the man, except for me. And Josh, who nobody seemed to have noticed.

'Come on,' Josh said, climbing the ladder up the side

of the hull.

They had stopped work with the bottom half of the cabin still in place, where the lockers were. Josh lay on the lid of the side-bed locker and disappeared, vanished.

Suddenly, I felt really cold and shivery. There was no way I was going to follow him into that locker.

'Come away, Nick,' Dad said quietly, 'the police are here. We caught the man, so they'll want to talk to you in a minute. But first—

'It's in the side-bed locker,' he said to the policeman who had followed him up the ladder. 'Don't look, Nick, it's not very nice.'

But I did look. There was a skeleton. Not a very big one. No bigger than mine would be with the muscles and sinews gone and the clothes rotted to rags. It was all bent up, with its knees in the air and threads of rope round the wrists and ankles.

They said it was probably a kidnapped boatboy, who had been kept prisoner. The boat had been sunk a hundred years or more, so there was no way of tracing who he was.

But I knew who it was from the catapult I'd seen lying beside the skeleton, near where its pocket would have been, with a pile of shiny blue pebbles.

It was Josh.

Humgruffin

Chloe Wolsey-Ottaway

Allow me to introduce myself: I am Dr Esther Weysol and this is my journal. I have been investigating Humgruffins for a number of years: I am the world expert on the subject. Humgruffin means 'a terrible person', but I think they are beasts, not people. These beasts live in every country, on every continent; but are so elusive that no one has ever managed to photograph one, let alone capture one.

Although I fear that a cornered Humgruffin may be extremely dangerous, I intend to discover one in its natural habitat, make detailed notes (which will be published as a bestselling book), then catch it and sell it to a zoo.

Humgruffrins have been confused with the Yeti, but they are *not* the same, for the Yeti is far too careless and allows itself to be spotted by anyone who happens to be in the vicinity. . .

From my research, the first thing that makes people suspect the presence of a Humgruffin is the discovery of large, unusual footprints; but they rarely leave those. Some hear loud, unexplained thwacks from the forest. Some say that wildflowers suddenly sprout through their lawns; others find their chickens running free in the morning. One lady swears a great shadow passed by her window, blocking out the moonlight for a second!

A Humgruffin is not the sort of creature you'd like to bump into, or have the misfortune to know. If you discovered one in the woods near your house, it would be best to move away as fast as you could pack up your belongings and get a removal van to take you!

Not so long ago, I met two Japanese children who insisted they had watched a Humgruffin bathing in a hot spring, but I found this extremely hard to believe. Even harder to believe, is that most adults doubt the Humgruffin exists at all, or that if he does, he is a stupid fellow. . . Please believe that he is very much alive and cunningly clever! I know, for I have seen a Humgruffin with my very own eyes. Well, his disappearing back, to be precise.

I shall continue to keep this important journal, adding a little every day, so that the world can later learn of my fascinating experiences and become further educated in the ways of these mysterious and dangerous beasts – the Humgruffins.

Tomorrow I fly to Peru, a land of wild terrain and amazing wildlife. Peru has mountains and forests, second to none. . . It is in Peru that I hope to get the first ever photographic evidence of a Humgruffin, if not the beast itself!

Peru Expedition: day one

I have arrived! Lima, the capital, is hot, dirty and busy. It took me *hours* to find a suitable guide with reliable transport, willing to take me and my supplies deep into the interior. The beaten-up jeep does not look reliable, I must say; it looks as if it should be put in a motor museum, or on a scrap heap. Tonight, I shall rest: we'll set off at dawn tomorrow. I am thrilled to be 'out in the field' once again!

Peru: day five

What a journey! I am aching and filthy, with a numb bottom, but delighted to have gotten this far. After travelling hundreds of bumpy miles on dangerous, pot-holed roads, my guide dropped me off beside a river, because there is no dusty track left to drive along. Waiting at the river was his cousin, with a motorboat. Tomorrow, we will go upriver.

Day seven

At last, I've set up my base-camp deep in the rainforest, further from civilisation than I've ever been before. My tent is pitched and my campfire lit. What an effort this expedition has been already! It's jolly difficult to find such remote spots now, because they're cutting down the forests so quickly.

In fact, this forest probably won't exist in twenty years; which is a pity, as it's as old as anything on earth and I've a hunch that undiscovered beasts lurk, hidden from human eyes. . . *All* forests are being chopped down at the same ferocious rate, so I hope to catch my Humgruffin before it's made extinct, along with everything else.

Day ten

I've set up six secret, infra-red wildlife cameras, which are triggered by movement to take pictures. I hope that an unsuspecting Humgruffin will stalk past in the dead of night, taking his own portrait, without even knowing it! Then I can set up a trap. So far, there's no signs of anything larger than nosy monkeys and the tracks of a jaguar.

Mosquitoes are the most trying aspect of living in the rainforest – I *loath* the little blighters! They bite me all day long, ignoring my state-of-the-art insect-repelling camouflaged clothing. At night, the little bloodsuckers feast upon me, even when I hide inside my deluxe mosquito net. I look like I have a shocking case of the measles.

Talking of bloodsuckers, I also *hate* yucky leeches, which get inside my boots, latch on to my skin and suck my blood until they're plump! I try to avoid water, but it's tricky, as this is a *rain*forest and my camp is beside the *river*!

Day thirty-blooming-two

Over a month has passed and still no luck! Every day, I search for endless miles and, at night, my cameras are ready and waiting. Almost everything I can imagine has taken its own picture, except the blasted Humgruffin – which is most vexing. It can't avoid me and my gizmos forever!

46

Bats got into my hair last night, making me trigger two of my own cameras by mistake: I took ridiculous pictures of myself, which will certainly *not* go into my book. How foolish! I'm considering leaving base-camp and following the river deeper into the rainforest, to try my luck there.

51

At last, a stroke of luck! This morning I found the huge footprints of a beast walking on two legs, with large claws and hairy toes. I'm thrilled! It's the most promising evidence yet, so I intend to follow the trail as far as I can. I'll take this journal, enough supplies for a fortnight, my cameras, my dictaphone and twenty little tapes to record any calls or noises a Humgruffin might make. I'm ready for him!

52

I, Esther Weysol, appear to be in quite a spot of bother.

Yesterday, I followed the trail until it disappeared into the river. An hour later, my usual powers of observation abandoned me, for I stupidly stepped into a snare and found myself suspended upside-down from a rope.

Out of the forest stepped the tallest, hairiest HUMGRUFFIN! I thought I was done for, as it looked furious. It snarled and growled as it cut me down.

However, it did not kill me. It tucked me under its hairy arm and carried me off to its den. I'm not quite sure what to do. . . In fact, there's not much I can do, as I'm locked in a cage, which is large enough for me to stand up in or lie down. Unfortunately, the cage is well constructed and I can't pick the lock.

The whole episode proves that I'm correct about the Humgruffin's intelligence and cunning.

All I can do is leave a clear record of what happens next. After all, I am a scientist and we scientists must keep our heads during unexpected events. First, I will describe the Humgruffin. As I said, he's almost eight feet tall and immensely strong, with a long, shaggy coat, which is a violet grey colour, like his eyes. The expression in his eyes is strangely sad, not murderous or savage, as I had assumed. The beast has uttered no words, only sighs or hums or grunts. I thought I heard what resembled a tune earlier but, of course, this couldn't be true.

The Humgruffin provided water and fruit, set down within my reach. And a blanket, made from its own fur, I think – which is just as well, because this cave is on the chilly side, despite the heat outside in the forest.

Now, I will stop for the day, as the Humgruffin

appears to be fascinated at what I am doing and I don't wish to have this journal taken away. The fright of being kidnapped has exhausted me. Dear reader, this may be my last ever entry, so I hope if this diary is ever found, that my efforts will be remembered and that I will be famous for taking great risks in the name of science . . .

Day 53

It's the end of an extraordinary day, which I will now record in detail, in case I forget any of it.

Against my worst expectations, I was not eaten for breakfast. Actually, I slept surprisingly well (considering my predicament) and awoke to the most extraordinary sight: the Humgruffin was feeding forest birds from its great, cupped hands! Whilst cooing softly!

Secretly, I switched on my dictaphone, to record the sound of the birds and his voice.

Next, the Humgruffin lifted a tiny jaguar cub from a deep nest of moss and fed it from a tiny bottle! A bottle!

'What's going on?!' I couldn't help exclaiming. (I have *every word* on tape, as evidence.)

'It's an orphan,' said the Humgruffin softly.

'WHAT?' I yelped, flabbergasted.

'Ssshh! You'll frighten her. A hunter killed her mother – she's alone,' whispered the Humgruffin.

'I know what an orphan is, thank you very much!' I snapped. 'It's just that. . .'

'Oh, of course – you're shocked because I'm speaking!'

the Humgruffin said, with a mischievous smile.

Which was exactly right, but I wasn't about to admit it and put myself at a disadvantage.

'I *demand* that you release me from this cage *immediately*,' I spluttered, in what I hoped was my most threatening voice. 'Kidnapping is against the law!'

'Yet you came to put me in a cage, did you not?' it asked simply.

'Well . . . umm . . . that's different,' I stammered, feeling most uncomfortable.

'Why is it different?' asked the Humgruffin reasonably.

'Because . . . because . . . well, I mean . . . because you're a **BEAST**!' I declared triumphantly. 'Humgruffins are dangerous, terrible monsters!'

'Are we really? Do you *know* any Humgruffins? What *exactly* do you know about what we do, or where we go?' he exclaimed.

'I know that you're . . . *secretive*,' I sniffed indignantly. 'Humans don't like not knowing what you're up to, that's what!'

I could hardly believe that a dangerous beast was questioning *me*!

'Humgruffins *have* to be secretive, because you humans are ruining everything,' the Humgruffin snarled, its huge face coming ever closer to my cage.

'Nonsense! We are not!' I said, outraged. 'How dare you!'

'The edges of my beautiful forest are being cut down,' he said. 'Can you deny it?'

'Umm . . . well . . .' was all I could think to say.

'Exactly! It is not just forests . . . It's the dzo, the manul, the mursu, the dugong and the teru-tero!'

'Oh, *what are you talking about*?' I exasperatedly sighed. 'I don't speak **Humgruffin**, you great buffoon!'

'It's English! They're the names of creatures you humans are killing off. . . They'll end up extinct, just like the poor dodos, passenger pigeons, great auks, quaggas and Mexican Grizzly bears! All sorts of wonderful creatures are in grave danger – like rhinos and elephants, wolves and whales.'

'I admit we might have been a tad thoughtless in the past,' I said shamefaced, unable to argue on this point.

'"In the past"?! it's happening *right now*!' said the Humgruffin, looking grim.

'Humans continue to hunt more than they need; they cut down trees without planting new ones; they fight terrible battles – killing each other. They keep multiplying, leaving less and less space for other living things.'

'Which is why you're very protective about the last, tiny strips of unspoiled land!' I exchanged.

'Exactly! Humgruffins are doing their best, but it's nearly too late. For even Humgruffins can't mend dead animals, or tend chopped-down forests. Without trees, we can't un-poison the seas and skies. . .'

'Nowadays, all we can do is rescue the last, or rare, creatures and collect the seeds of disappearing plants. We bring them to the last remote places, hoping to save them. But soon, even we Humgruffins will become extinct, or die of sorrow. What are we to do?'

★

For the first time in my life, I, the eminent scientist, Dr Esther Weysol, did not have an answer. I had been entirely wrong about Humgruffins for years – they are not terrible beasts. In fact, they are wise and kind.

'Humgruffin, there *is* something we can do. . . Come back with me and tell everyone about Humgruffins and what can be done to save our planet.'

'Will anyone listen?' said the Humgruffin.

'Yes, they will!'

The End

(Or is it just a new beginning?)

The Monsters' Bus

Shane O'Hara

Sgt Cudgel had come across some strange things during his time in the police, but nothing quite as strange as the story that Mrs Henry had told him. Mrs Henry claimed her friend, Doris Bloom, had been abducted by a ghostly bus. 'We'd been to the Town Hall dance, you see,' she said. 'It didn't finish till after nine, and then the bus was late. By the time it appeared, Doris couldn't wait to get on.' Mrs Henry sniffled and dabbed her eyes with a hanky as she spoke. 'I said to her, hang on, Doris, I don't like the look of that bus – it's *glowing*. But she didn't care. She just wanted to get home for a cup of tea. Well, she jumped straight on – I tried to hold her back, but she wouldn't have it. I just caught sight of the driver and *ooh*, shivers ran down my spine! He had this big hood pulled up over his head. When Doris saw him she screamed and tried to get off, but the doors shut with her trapped inside. I can still see her face pressed against the glass as it drove away!'

Sgt Cudgel sighed. Mrs Henry was getting on a bit – perhaps she had dreamt it? 'Why didn't you come to us straightaway?' he asked.

'I did – I phoned the police station and the young man I spoke to told me to go home and get some rest, and everything would be all right in the morning. Everyone thinks you're mad when you get older. But I'm *not* mad – I know what happened to Doris!'

Sgt Cudgel shifted uncomfortably in his seat. *Everyone thinks you're mad when you get older.* The words rang in his ears and he felt ashamed. Then he had an idea. 'I think I know someone who may be able to help,' he said.

Sgt Cudgel left the interview room and picked up a phone.

'Hello, Civic Centre? Can you put me through to extension 2040? Thanks.'

The phone rang twice until a man with a bright voice answered.

'Supernatural Pests department, Arthur Von Trappenstoppen speaking. How may I help you?'

'Morning, Arthur. It's Sgt Cudgel here. Could you come down to the station? We've got a lady in a right state here – keeps going on about a glowing bus that kidnapped her friend last night. We've drawn a blank, I'm afraid. Nothing showing up on the CCTV. It sounds like it might be one for you.'

'Hmmm. A glowing bus? Sounds interesting. I'll be right over.' Sgt Cudgel put down the phone. Arthur had helped him before, and he just hoped he could help him now.

Arthur Von Trappenstoppen arrived at the station and reported to the front desk. He was a tall, thin man with a long, almost comical, face. But the face was also honest, sincere and brave – though not many people saw that; Arthur kept it well hidden.

In the interview room, Arthur listened patiently as Mrs Henry told her story. 'Honestly,' she said, 'it gave me such a fright. I don't know what public transport is coming too. It's an outrage!'

'Well,' said Sgt Cudgel, 'what do you think?'

'I think you were right to call me. This has definite supernatural overtones. Leave it with me, Mrs Henry. I'll find your friend.'

That evening, Arthur waited at the same bus-stop that Mrs Bloom and Mrs Henry had done the night before.

Around his waist he wore a big brown belt, which had a number of large pockets and attachments. This was his equipment belt, and he never went on an investigation without it.

Arthur tapped his watch to check it was still running. The bus was late. Arthur glanced in the opposite direction for a moment and when he looked back he was surprised to see a glowing bus coming toward his stop. 'Fascinating,' whispered Arthur as the bus approached. It made no noise; instead it silently glided toward the bus-stop where Arthur waited. The bus drew to a halt and its doors opened.

And there, just as Mrs Henry had described, was the hooded driver. Arthur hopped on to the bus. The driver reached out towards him, revealing a white skeletal hand. Quickly, Arthur dropped a pound coin into those bony fingers.

'Just as far as Oakley Road, please,' he said, acting as if all bus drivers looked like this one did. The hooded figure dropped the coin into the cash box and out popped a ticket. 'Thank you,' smiled Arthur as he took the ticket.

The doors closed and the bus started to move.

Arthur walked down the bus and eyed his fellow passengers. His suspicions that this was a bus of supernatural origin were confirmed.

Sat on the left, reading a newspaper, was a large werewolf. 'Evening,' he growled.

On the right, a few seats down, sat two mummies. They stopped chatting as Arthur walked by and nodded politely in his direction. Still further down was a big green demon. He glanced at Arthur but didn't say anything. Opposite the demon sat a vampire. She was knitting and far too busy to take any notice of anything else. Arthur made his way to the very back of the bus, and there he found Mrs Bloom. She looked tired and frightened, and trembled a little as Arthur approached and sat next to her. Her eyes widened as Arthur learned towards her. 'Don't worry,' he whispered, 'I'm from the Council. I've come to take you home.'

Mrs Bloom gave a huge sign of relief. 'Oh, thank goodness! These things won't let me get off! And I'm dying for a cup of tea.'

'Try to relax,' replied Arthur. 'I'll have you off this bus as soon as I can. I need you to stay calm, no matter what happens next. OK?' Mrs Bloom nodded.

As the bus travelled along, various creatures got on and off.

A troll got on, fumbled for change, and got off two stops later.

A ghostly figure floated on, hovered above a seat and got off at the next stop. Finally, another hooded figure got on to the bus.

He started to walk down the bus, stopping at the werewolf.

'Tickets, please,' he said in a low, moanful voice. The werewolf handed over his ticket for inspection. The hooded figure looked at it carefully then, satisfied, handed it back. Arthur watched as the hooded figure moved on to the two mummies and inspected their tickets, then on to the demon.

Arthur leaned over to Mrs Bloom and whispered

again, 'Things may start to get a little . . . raucous soon. Just stay close to me.'

'Don't you worry,' replied Mrs Bloom 'I'm not letting you out of my sight!'

The hooded inspector checked the vampire's ticket and then he came to Arthur and Doris. 'Tickets, please,' he moaned.

Arthur smiled and handed over his ticket.

The inspector gazed at the ticket. Then raised his hooded head and looked at Arthur.

'This isn't right,' he said. 'You're not one of us . . . you're a HUMAN!'

This sentence was shouted out so everyone on the bus could hear. A gasp went up from the other passengers and they all turned to stare at Arthur.

'Actually,' said Arthur, calmly standing to face the sinister inspector, 'I'm from the council's Supernatural Pests department. And I have to tell you that you are in violation of at least six council by-laws, plus a very serious offence of holding Mrs Bloom here on your bus against her will.'

'Whaaaattt!' wailed the inspector, 'We don't care about your Human laws! You will be our prisoner along with that Woman – you will *never* leave this bus!' The inspector turned to the passengers and raised his arms. 'GET HIM!' he shouted. The monstrous passengers leapt from their seats and moved menacingly up the bus towards Arthur and Mrs Bloom.

The hooded inspector made a grab for Arthur, but Arthur dodged aside and gave him a shove that sent him flying down the bus. The werewolf sprang forward, growling and snapping.

Arthur quickly reached into his belt and pulled out a steel cylinder. 'Here, boy,' he shouted. 'FETCH!' He hurled the cylinder into the air. The werewolf couldn't help himself. Suddenly behaving like a puppy, he leapt up and caught the shiny spinning object in his toothy mouth. Landing nimbly on two paws, the werewolf gave a satisfied grunt.

'Good boy. . .' said Arthur, '. . . and goodbye!' The werewolf's eyes opened with surprise as the cylinder cracked open and erupted into a ball of searing orange light.

The light flared up and out, engulfing the hairy beast in its brilliance. Then, with a loud pop, the light vanished, along with one very perplexed werewolf.

The hooded inspector roared out in fury and shook a bony fist!

'DESTROY HIM! TEAR HIM LIMB FROM LIMB! HE'S FROM THE COUNCIL!'

The two mummies, who had seemed so pleasant earlier on, now rushed forward.

Arthur pulled two small sticky cubes from his belt and threw them at the mummies. They gave each other a confused look as the cubes landed on them with a sticky splat – and then the shaking started. It began gently, but within seconds the mummies were shaking so hard that bits of bandage started to fly off them.

'OOOHHH! HELP!' they wailed, but it was no good.

The mummies shook and shook, faster and faster. Soon, they were shaking so hard that they could hardly be seen, their figures becoming blurry and faint.

Moments later, all that remained of the ancient horrors were two little piles of sand on the floor.

'Oh, you handled that well,' exclaimed Mrs Bloom, full of admiration. Arthur blushed a little. 'Oh, er, thank you. Nice of you to say.'

The remaining monsters were not amused.

'OOH, That's it!' wailed the inspector. 'Now you've really done it! Now I'm mad! Now you will PAY!' He turned to the green demon and the vampire, 'Attack! Destroy him and I'll see to it that you get free travel for a week!' The demon and the vampire clearly thought that this was a very good offer, because they both rushed towards Arthur. In fact, they rushed forward so quickly that neither looked where the other was going and, in their haste to destroy the council-man first, they got jammed in the aisle between the seats.

'Do excuse me, Mrs Bloom,' said Arthur, dashing forward towards the struggling pair.

The demon slashed out with its huge claws; Arthur ducked, reached into his belt and pulled out a handful of pink dust.

The vampire hissed and snapped with her fangs, while the demon struck out again, its claws just missing Arthur's head as he dodged away. Turning quickly, Arthur threw the dust into the snarling demon's face! The demon stopped. Its nose twitched. And twitched again. Arthur hurried back to Mrs Bloom.

'You might want to get behind the seat, Mrs Bloom,' suggested Arthur, gently pushing her down. The demon's nose was now twitching furiously and the vampire, still trapped between him and the seat, didn't like it at all. She struggled to get free but was stuck fast. The demon took a deep breath, then another still deeper. His eyes were watering and he was clearly building up to something. The vampire whimpered, knowing that there was no escape, and then . . .

'AAAA-CHHOOOOOOO!!!!'

The green demon sneezed so hard that he exploded, taking the vampire with him!

★

The bus shook as a shock wave ripped through it, and huge chunks of green gunge flew through the air splattering against the seats, windows and floor. The bus veered wildly across the road as the driver made an emergency stop.

Arthur and Mrs Bloom popped up from behind the seat, which was covered with gunge. 'Oh dear,' tutted

Mrs Bloom, 'This is going to take a while to clear up.' At the front of the bus, the inspector stood dripping from hooded head to bony foot in green slime.

He was making a sort of low, helpless blubbing noise as he tried to brush the gooey mess off him. 'In all my years,' he blubbed, 'in all my years of working on the monsters' bus I've never known anything like this!'

He slumped down on to one of the slime-covered seats, dejectedly holding his hooded head in his bony white hands. The driver, also covered in green goo, struggled out from the driving seat and stood over the inspector, gently laying his hand on his shoulder for comfort. 'Come on,' said Arthur to Mrs Bloom, 'time for us to go.'

They walked quickly to the door, past the inspector and driver. The driver made a half-hearted attempt to grab them, but the inspector stopped him. 'Oh, just let them go,' he murmured. 'I'll be glad to be rid of them!'

Arthur helped Mrs Bloom safely off the bus. 'Just wait here for me, would you? I've one more thing to do.' He went back to the bus door and shouted inside. 'Er, sorry to be a nuisance, but this is for you.' With a graceful lob he threw a small silver ball inside. The driver caught it just as the inspector looked up.

'Oh, no,' he moaned weakly. The driver and inspector looked in stunned silence as the ball burst open in a shattering blast of energy that engulfed the bus, beams of sizzling light springing and zigzagging up and down the aisle until the spooky vehicle began to crumple and fold, turning in on itself a like a piece of paper, scrunching and crushing until it vanished completely.

'There,' said Arthur, dusting his hands as he walked back to Mrs Bloom. 'I don't believe they will be troubling anyone again.'

Mrs Bloom was very relieved. She straightened her coat and adjusted her handbag. 'Oh, thank you so much. I can't tell you how grateful I am. Mind, I'll be writing a strong letter of complain to the Bus Company.'

Arthur smiled. 'My car's parked just round the corner. Could I give you a lift home? And, if you don't mind, I wonder if you would fill in this customer satisfaction survey when you have a moment? Some of the Councillors are very keen on this sort of thing.'

Arthur drove Mrs Bloom home, where Mrs Henry was waiting. Mrs Bloom finally got the cup of tea she had wanted for so long, drinking as she told her friend of everything that had happened. 'I do hope that this little incident won't put you off going to the Town Hall dance,' said Arthur.

'Not likely,' replied Mrs Bloom. 'It takes more than a glowing bus and few unkempt monsters to keep us away, hey, Winifred?'

Arthur left the two old friends chatting as he drove off into the night, happy with another job well done.

Alice and the Alien

Heather Black

It was the last day of school term and Alice charged towards home. Freedom. Seven weeks of freedom to be precise. Seven weeks of playing on the rocks and swimming in the Firth with Morag.

Morag was Alice's best friend – they were 'joined at the hip', her mum said. Adults were weird!

Alice and her parents lived in Bothy Cottage. Her mum was an artist who painted pictures of Croftie Loch for the tourists. They paid a lot of money for Mum's pictures. Very few people bought Alice's though. Even though her mum told her she was 'a natural'.

Alice burst through the door and kicked off her shoes, her bag slid along the floor into the dining-room, and with the skill of a basketball player, she threw her coat neatly over the knob of the sitting-room door. Home.

'Mum . . . I'm home!' Alice bellowed.

No answer? Alice's face puckered, her eyebrows forming two perfect question marks.

'Muuuuummmm . . . I'm hooooome!!!' Alice squealed.

There were no mum sounds from anywhere inside

the house. Alice opened the back door and she spotted her mum blethering to Old Mrs Stewart at the bottom of the garden. Mrs Stewart and her mum were *always* blethering. Dad said that Mrs Stewart was a better information service than 'News at Ten'.

'Yes, I agree, Mrs Stewart,' said Alice's mum quietly 'It does seem odd. Alien really.'

'Well, mark my words, Jane. I don't know who planned it, but it does not seem like a sensible thing to me. Moving them to Croftie Loch is very odd.' Mrs Stewart sucked in the air as if she were thirsty for breath. 'Where are they from, again?'

'Azerbaijan, I think,' replied Alice's mum.

Alice appeared magically from behind her dad's striped pyjamas that were hanging on the washing-line. Her freckled nose twitched and she scooped her curly red hair away from her face. She eyed the pair curiously.

'Oh hello, Alice hen,' said Old Mrs Stewart.

Alice nodded politely, her eyes flicking from one woman to the other like ping- pong balls.

'Alice darling. How was your day?'

'Fine thanks, Mum.' (*Until now*, thought Alice.) 'I'm . . . going . . . to get . . . em . . . changed. Then . . . I'm away for . . . em . . . Morag.'

Alice's mum smiled fondly and wondered why her daughter was stuttering.

Alice escaped from the two women and bounded the stairs to her room two at a time. She squirmed into her jeans, threw a T-shirt over her head, slipped trainers on to her feet, a biscuit into her mouth, a carton of orange into her hand and charged away again.

Morag stared, her wide eyes peeping over the top of her round rimmed spectacles. Morag had short brown hair, cut into a bob, which her mum had said was very trendy. Alice wanted trendy hair too, but her scarlet curls 'had a mind of their own'. So Alice just kept her hair in a pony tail, which was 'much more practical'.

'Are you sure that's what she said, Alice?' Morag whispered.

Alice scanned the empty beach for signs of intruders, 'I was standing behind the pyjama legs, so that's why they didn't see me. My mum said "Aliens really?" Then Mrs Stewart said that she didn't know "why they were moving to Croftie Loch" or "whose planet" they were from and my mum said "Ishabaja".'

Morag took Alice's hands, 'I've never heard of that planet before ,Alice. When we studied "The Milky Way" do you remember Mr Jones talking about a planet called Ishabaja?'

'I know about Pluto and Saturn and Mars,' Alice sighed and looked up at the sky in wonder, 'but not that one. This has to be our secret, Morag. Until we find out more about the aliens *and* where they are living.'

Alice and Morag spent the rest of the evening planning their 'mission'. Tomorrow, they would check in at the Black Rock on the beach. Morag would bring the binoculars and Alice a pen and notepad. Both needed to bring food and drink, because this 'investigation' might take a while said Morag.

The next morning, Alice woke up really early. She dressed in black trousers and a black top. She found a pair of her mum's old sunglasses and popped them into her rucksack beside the pen and notepad. She squeezed her unbrushed ponytail under a black baseball cap until it seemed to burst at the seams.

'Good morning, Alice,' her mum smiled, 'Hungry?'

Alice looked at her mum and nodded. 'But . . . I'll get it myself thanks, Mum . . . just some cereal . . . em . . . and I'll take some snacks for my picnic with Morag.'

Alice's mum smiled again and left the kitchen. 'Have a nice day, sweetheart,' she shouted back. 'Don't do anything I wouldn't do.'

What a cheek, thought Alice. It wasn't her who was hiding the fact that aliens were living in Croftie Loch!

At Black Rock, Morag was already there, scanning the Firth with her dad's binoculars, every now and again turning them towards the sky, as if she were expecting something to drop from a cloud. She saw Alice and waved.

'Ready?' she said.

'Yep!' Alice nodded.

The girls planned in careful stages. Stage 1 – find out where the aliens lived. Morag said that Croftie Loch was so small any strangers would stick out like a sore thumb. Especially strangers with green faces and two heads, Alice replied.

Alice pulled the notepad and pen from her bag, sat on the rocks and wrote:

Day 1
Today's mishion – find out where THEY live.

Both girls marvelled at their plan. Alice tucked loose strands of hair back under her cap and she popped the oversized sunglasses on to her face. Her disguise was complete.

Walking from the beach, they headed to town, eeling through the streets; peeking round each corner before slipping on, towards the church.

They turned into Boatyard Place and stopped! There, on the left-hand side of the street stood an enormous silver cube. It had six round tyre-shaped landing shoes, and on the side was writing. Very unusual writing . Alice grabbed the pen and wrote:

First sighting – 10.13 a.m. Big silver spaceship found in Boatyard Place. Strange code on side, HorowitzerFrankenspeil, 203445 Gunther Straasen, Heerenveen 4073 Bruxelles. Transportation Extraordinaire.

Morag looked at Alice and Alice looked at Morag. Both girls were unusually silent. Then Morag whispered, 'That is definitely an alien name, Alice. Why d'ya think there's no Ishabaja on the side too? *If* that's where they are from,' she stressed.

Alice looked at her friend, shook her head in disgust, and spat through gritted teeth, 'Because, you idiot, they don't want us to find out that they are aliens, do they? I mean, they're not going to put an advert in the *Daily Record* to let us know they're here – Doh!'

Morag flushed, embarrassed. *Alice really was clever*, she thought.

The next day, the girls arranged to meet at the church. Armed with the binoculars, notepad and pen, they set about the next stage of the plan.

Day 2
Find out what they look like.

The spaceship had gone when the girls arrived. Morag said it had probably lifted off in the night when the town was asleep. The girls glanced at the sky, and then at each other. Morag grabbed Alice's hand,

'I'm a wee bit scared, Alice. What if they eat humans?'

'Listen, Morag, nobody in this town screams louder than me and you. If they try to eat us then we'll just have to scream. OK?'

Morag chewed her bottom lip nervously and nodded.

The girls set up their viewpoint at the top of the churchyard, behind the older tombstones. From there they could see the whole of Boatyard Place, and all the comings and goings. Alice and Morag were becoming very skilled detectives. Move over Mulder and Scully, Alice said; Morag agreed, but wondered what Jack Brown's hamsters had to do with this.

It was nearly lunch-time when the first signs of alien activity began.

First sighting – 11.51 a.m. Small boy-shaped alien out in garden. He is throwing a round white ball-shaped object. Could be a weapon.

Alice peeped over the wall. The alien looked normal. Like a real human; just a different colour to most humans Alice had seen before. Morag joined her friend and looked through the binoculars, 'I'm not being funny, Alice, but doesn't that white thing look like a ball?'

'It does look a bit like a ball,' Alice nodded, 'but how would an alien know how to play football?'

'Maybe they've been watching us for a long time before they came.'

Alice smiled at her friend. She was quite wise from time to time; Morag.

Suddenly, another alien appeared from the house. This time it was a woman alien with a baby alien in her arms. She handed the boy alien a sandwich and popped the baby into a strange-looking green capsule with wheels. It looked a bit like Alice's old pram. Alice and Morag were confused.

'He's eating a sandwich, Alice. If he eats sandwiches, then that means he won't be eating us for pudding. D'ya think?'

'For once, Morag, I think you could be right. Maybe they are nice aliens. My mum didn't seem scared when she was talking about them.'

The girls decided that they had discovered enough for one day, and went for a swim in the Bluewell Burn. Alien investigations could wait until tomorrow.

On the third day, Alice and Morag arranged to meet in the afternoon. This way they could have a lie-in. They knew where the aliens lived now, and today was to be the most important day so far.

Day 3
First Contact.

Alice grabbed her usual supply of crisps, biscuits and cans of coke, but this time she added something else to her rucksack – her dad's book on the Solar System. Every planet in the Milky Way was there and Alice was determined to find Ishabaja today.

Morag was waiting for Alice at the old tombstone. She, too, had put on sunglasses today; worried that the aliens may be able to read her mind. The glasses would stop them seeing into her brain and sucking her thoughts. Morag shuddered. She had scared herself.

The two girls waited, watching the aliens' house. It wasn't long before the boy alien appeared with his round object again. He kicked it around the garden. He dribbled it with his feet. He bounced it off the window.

The woman alien came out and shouted a few loud words, which Morag and Alice did not understand, but she pointed at the little alien using her finger in the exact same way as Alice's mum did when Alice was in trouble. He was looking at his feet; just the same as Alice did.

'She's telling him off,' whispered Morag.

'Look, he's crying,' replied Alice.

'What colour are his tears, Alice?'

Alice picked up the binoculars and looked at the boy alien's face. It was all puckered up as if he'd sucked a gooseberry. As Alice focused in on his face, she saw that his tears were see- through.

'They're see-through tears, Morag. Just like mine and yours.'

'D'ya think we should see if he's OK? I mean, he doesn't seem all that scary to me.'

The two girls scraped over the churchyard wall and dropped to the soft earth at the other side. Slowly, they approached the little boy alien. He saw them coming and wiped his face, eyeing them blankly.

Alice noticed that his eyes were really dark. He

looked the same age as Alice and Morag, about nine or ten. Alice stepped forward and held her hand up in a sign of peace. She gave the alien her widest grin.

'Welcome to Earth,' she said proudly. 'Peace!'

Morag stared at Alice in amazement. Her friend was truly amazing. She knew how to make contact with aliens. The little alien looked even more bewildered, but smiled back.

'Which – plaaanet – aare – youuu – frommmm?' Alice spoke each word at twenty-second intervals. 'Thisss – isss – Eaaarth. – Youuu – aaare – innn – Scooootlaaand'.

Morag, dumbfounded at her friend's skill, watched as the alien repeated the word 'Scotland'. He smiled happily. Morag noticed his teeth were like hers; not pointy or pink or anything else odd. Just like human teeth.

Alice suddenly took off, running across the street like a racehorse. She jumped the wall and disappeared. Morag and the alien stared after her. As quickly as she'd disappeared, Alice was back, carrying a great big black book, with the words 'Planets of the Universe' on the front. She placed the book on the grass beside the little alien, opened the book at page 51 and pointed.

'Earth. This is Earth. I am an Earthling called Alice. This is an Earthling called Morag.' She poked her friend.

Morag had never been called an Earthling before, but it sounded very important, so she liked it. She too pointed to the picture and to herself, repeating the words, 'Earth, Morag. Earthling'.

Alice tutted, frowning at Morag, but said nothing. The little alien smiled at them both, and vanished into the house. Alice and Morag stood in bemused silence. When he returned a few minutes later, he too was carrying a large book in his hands.

On the front of the book, were the words 'Atlas of the World'. The little alien opened up the Atlas and scanned through the book until he came to a page that made him smile. He pointed to the map and declared 'Azerbaijan. Home'.

That summer, Alice, Morag and Ismail became very good friends. The girls were relieved to discover their new friend was not an alien after all, but was going to be the newest member of their school.

Alice never did find out why her mum thought Ismail and his family were aliens. She did know, however, that adults were weird!

The Thought-Bee

Anne Wehrle

Have you ever wanted to know what someone else was thinking? To get inside their head, have a little nose around at the scenery, and shine a torch into the hidden corners of their mind, without them even knowing? Well, a few months ago, I got the chance to do exactly that. And it turned out to be a very illuminating experience indeed.

It all started with one of those conversations I've found myself having more and more often with my mum recently – where I keep repeating 'Oh *pur-leeeze*, Mum,' in the whiniest, most annoying voice I can muster, and then wait patiently for her to stop saying no and agree. The object of my desire in this instance was one of those little egg-shaped toys you find in bubble-vending machines outside newsagents. The egg contains a toy and, if you're lucky, some chocolate or sweets. That's what I like so much about them: that element of surprise, of never quite knowing what you might discover inside.

Finally, (because she is pretty well trained, by now, my mum) she gave in and starting searching in her purse while simultaneously shaking her head, rolling her eyes at me and giving one of her melodramatic 'What did I do to deserve this child?' sighs. I skipped outside, placed the money in the slot and turned the chunky handle with a satisfying tug. The yellow egg plopped out and sat in the shiny recess.

I trailed up the road behind Mum, clasping the egg to me like a precious jewel. If anyone had passed me by, they would have seen a young girl wandering along in a daydream, but I was in fact very busy trying to guess what might be hidden inside the egg. Would it be an animal? I hoped so. Maybe a cute koala bear or a giraffe with a bendable neck? If not, how about a necklace or some nail stickers? I definitely didn't want a racing car or a key- ring, but a puzzle wouldn't be so bad.

One thing's for sure, when I finally allowed myself to look inside, I certainly got the surprise I was after.

And what a surprise it turned out to be.

The first sign that something was amiss was when I shook the egg to give myself a clue. Strange. It felt extremely light, as if there was nothing in it at all.

But then I heard it.

An almost imperceptible buzzing sound was coming from inside the egg. I cradled it in my palm and held it up to my ear. Yes, there was definitely something moving in there. How weird! It must be some kind of mechanical toy. But why was it already going off? And why did it feel so light?

Back home, in the privacy of my bedroom, I slowly prised the two sides of the egg apart. As I did so, I could feel the buzzing intensify, as if the toy had a mind of its own and was banging against the sides of the egg, eager to get out.

There, curled up inside the egg, was a solitary slip of paper. It looked suspiciously like the type you'd normally find inside a cracker, with some lame joke on it. Intrigued, I pulled it out and, sure enough, there was the joke.

I'm your private Thought-bee
Be sure to use me carefully;
Put somebody's name inside me
And I will tell you what they see;
You can use me daily
But I will not last eternally.

What on earth did that mean? I wondered. It certainly wasn't a joke, but sounded more like a riddle. One that made no sense to me. And where was my toy? Or at least some chocolate? Just my luck to get the only dud egg in the machine!

Hang on a minute, the other side of my brain interrupted. What was making the buzzing sound? There *was* something else inside the egg.

I lay on my bed staring at the ceiling, and puzzled over it. Bees buzz. The riddle says it's my private

Thought-bee. Whatever a Thought-bee is. Bumble-bee, yes. Thought-bee, no. Where exactly is this bee, anyway? Did it fly off before I even got the chance to see it? And what does it mean by *I will tell you what they see*? Would I actually be able to see people's thoughts?

After much debate, the two sides of my brain finally came to an agreement. I would put someone's name inside the egg, as instructed. And then wait to see what happened.

★

I figured that if the egg was going to tell me what someone was thinking, then I'd better pick someone who was in the house. Daniel was out playing football, which left Mum. So that, at least, was an easy decision. I duly wrote *Mum* on a scrap of paper torn from my homework diary, and then added *Gloria* as an afterthought. (There are quite a few mums in the world, after all.)

I placed it in the empty egg, feeling a mixture of excitement, trepidation and complete stupidity, slammed the two sides of it back together, laid it carefully on my bed and waited for something to happen.

And waited . . .

and waited . . .

Nothing happened. Now I just felt stupid. I'm not sure what I'd expected: a flash of light, or a voice booming into my room, maybe?

Wait a second. What if you had to be holding the egg

for it to work? The instructions weren't exactly clear. I picked the egg back up and closed my eyes tight, waiting for my mum's thoughts to come sailing into my head.

Nothing.

I opened my eyes and glanced around me. What a fool for believing it might actually work! I mean, fancy thinking an egg would be able to read people's minds! I must be going mad. Dumb egg! What a waste of money. I picked it up and hurled it into the corner of my room.

★

That night, I dreamt of a giant newly-hatched egg chasing me on its side like a massive mouth, with egg white dripping out from between its sharp teeth like saliva, while I tried to run away with legs that kept collapsing on me, as if they were made of jelly. Just as it was about to swallow me whole, the egg became a swarm of bees that circled me angrily, their buzzing growing louder and louder the closer they came.

Emerging hazily from this dangerous world to find myself safely tucked up in bed, it was a few minutes before I realised that the buzzing sound was actually real and it was coming from the other side of my bedroom.

I stumbled over to where I'd thrown the egg the previous evening, and retrieved it from amongst a pile of my dirty washing. It was buzzing so hard, it looked like it was moving and the vibrations tickled my fingers as I picked it up.

I yanked it open and found not only the scrap of

paper I'd placed so hopefully in it the night before, but also another, bigger piece of paper. I unfolded it and, wiping sleep from my eyes, read the following:

The tumble drier's broken
Hang the washing on the line
What with hoovering and ironing
I just don't have the time;
Work again tomorrow
Got that document to write
Parents' evening after school
Hope Danny's done all right;
Burgers, chips and beans
Will have to do for the kids' tea
Has Katie done her homework?
When will I have time for me?

Had it really worked? These must have been my mum's thoughts last night. The Thought-bee had done what it said it would! I read it again. That's exactly what we had for tea last night. *And* Daniel's got parents' evening tonight. But what's she worrying about my homework for? Of course I've done it. Well, most of it, anyway.

What was it the rhyme had said? *You can use me once a day* or something like that. Well, if it had the power to read minds, then I was going to have to find some more exciting minds to read. Today was a new day. Who should I choose next? I'd have to wait until I got to school, unless I wanted to find out what my little brother spent his time thinking about, but I was sure it would just be Pokemon or his latest stupid craze.

As soon as I arrived through the gates I spotted my target. Miss Plant. Year Six teacher. Perfect.

She'd be sure to have more interesting thoughts than my mum. What gossip could I glean from her? I wondered. Scandal in the staffroom? Snippets about students? I would soon be able to find out.

I scribbled her name and put it in the egg, under the cover of the table, wondering as I did so, how exactly this thing worked. I pictured a bee so tiny that you couldn't actually see it, weaving its way across the classroom before entering Miss Plant's domed head through her ear as she droned on about our terrible behaviour. I watched her carefully, but she didn't seem like a woman who had a foreign object in her head. No more so than usual, anyway.

I wasn't sure how long I should wait before opening the egg back up again; I didn't want to do it too early in case it somehow ruined the process.

By breaktime, though, it had started to buzz again, so I took this as a sign that it had done its job. I slipped into the girls' toilets and gingerly opened the egg. *Bingo!* There was another poem inside it:

Literacy, assembly,
Numeracy then art
Remember during breaktime
On the board to draw maths chart;
They've understood the homework
Though I've still got to check on Miles
At lunch I'll get some marking done
Got to work my way through piles;
Who's that person talking?
And is Katie passing notes?
Must make an appointment at the doctor
All this shouting hurts my throat.

How tedious can you get? If this is the way adults think then I don't ever want to grow old! At least children think about interesting things, like why the sky is blue and not yellow, and why cats have nine lives when dogs only get one.

My next Thought-bee sting was going to have to be someone in my class. Step in Billy Kane, love of my life (except he hardly knows I exist). I could find out if he secretly liked me too, or if he was going to be at Becky's party on Saturday.

Only trouble was I was gong to have to wait until the next day to find out.

*

Wednesday seemed to take years to arrive but, when it finally did, and the buzzing signalled it was ripe for reading, this is what the bee told me about his thoughts:

We had our game cut short at breaktime
The ball was lobbed over the fence
I'll tell Ross to go up front at lunch
'Cause I play better in defence;
Ben is bringing his Playstation
When he comes round after school
Rally Driver is his best game
But James Bond is also cool.

Right, OK, so parents, teachers and boys all think dull thoughts. What about girls? Surely their thoughts must be just slightly more interesting? What would my best friend Becky be thinking? Probably nothing she hadn't already told me, because she tells me everything, as best friends should. Still, hers was Thursday's name in the egg:

Just can't wait until my party
Got to find something to wear
Off to shops with Kate on Saturday
How shall I wear my hair?
I'm not inviting Smelly Kelly
'Cause I don't like that girl one bit
But the guest of honour's coming:
Billy Kane – he's just sooooo fit!

Well, so much for being BFs. Not only had she not told me who she fancied, he was the very boy she knew that I was mad about! I wasn't sure I would be going shopping with her on Saturday, after all. What else had she been keeping from me?

Friday's victim was a hard choice. Who would be thinking fascinating thoughts? Who could provide me with some light entertainment? I searched the classroom for a suitable candidate. No boring boys or teachers. It would have to be another girl.

And there she was. I don't know why it took me so long. Kelly Judd, also known as Smelly Kelly. She was the class pain, the one who everyone said had nits. The one who tried to run away from school when we were in Year Three. The one who spent most playtimes by herself. What in the world would be going on in her head? Time to find out:

Got to do the shopping after school
Mum's in hospital again;
I hate my life, the class hate me
Why can't I be like them?
Hope that Dad stays out tonight
'Cause he gets violent on the drink
No good telling anyone at school
I know what they all think.

Well, you can imagine how I felt then. Pretty ashamed of myself, if the truth be known. There was me, so wrapped up in my own petty problems, willing to join in with the rest of the class in being nasty to Kelly, without knowing anything about her life, and without giving a second thought to how she might be feeling.

The Thought-bee stopped working after that. I was a bit disappointed I never got a chance to read the dog's mind, but it had warned me it wouldn't last for ever, I suppose. In fact, the more I thought about it, the more it seemed like the Thought-bee had been waiting for me to choose Kelly. As if it had had a job to do and, once it had completed its job, that was it. Although I'm sure the bee's now long gone, I've kept the egg as a souvenir, and to remind me that I really don't have a clue what other people might be thinking.

Kelly's never asked me why I suddenly started sticking up for her, but then I doubt she'd believe me if I told her the truth. She sometimes comes round after school and we often do our homework together. I've discovered that she owns a guinea-pig, two rabbits and a hamster. We're even going to the same secondary school in September.

I don't spend much time with Becky these days, though. She spends all her time with her new boyfriend, Billy. And he spends all his time talking to her about football.

How romantic.

The MGF

Clair Matthews

'Daniel!!!' The high-pitched screech ripped through the house like a tornado, causing Dan to freeze in his seat at the computer, the hairs on the back of his neck shooting up like soldiers standing to attention. What had he done now? It must be pretty serious: mum only called him Daniel when she was extremely annoyed with him.

'DANIEL JACKSON, GET HERE NOW!' – things were getting worse. Dan had discovered over the years that the more syllables his mum used when calling his name the deeper the trouble he was in. He had better get to her quickly before she added his middle name!

Dan ran down the hallway, sprinted through the lounge (narrowly missing a potentially fatal collision with the sofa) and reached the kitchen in five seconds flat, a new personal record. He looked at his mother, his face a vision of innocence; 'Did you want me?'

His mother stood in front of the kitchen sink, the bubbles from the washing-up still clinging to her hands and arms. Next to her, with a face as red as a cherry tomato, stood his younger sister Charlotte, more affectionately known as Lottie, not that affection was something that Dan ever associated with her. Lottie was sobbing uncontrollably, tears running down her puffy cheeks.

Dan waited for his mother to say something, anything. Experience had taught him that in these situations it was probably best for him to keep quiet. After a long silence, during which his mother just stared at him, breathing deeply and looking very much like a dragon just before it unleashes a powerful jet of flames from its nostrils, she spoke.

'Would you like to tell me your side of the story?' she asked, her voice sounding noticeably strained. And then, without waiting for a reply, she launched into a full- on attack. 'Lottie said that you practically threw her out of the office. She only wanted to watch you on the computer. Honestly, Daniel, how could you be so mean? After all, she's only five years old and you're nearly eleven! You should know better. Look at the state she's in. I don't know what I'm going to do with you.'

Dan watched his mother in disbelief, how could anybody possibly give a speech like that without even drawing breath? As if in response to this thought, his mother paused and breathed in, a sharp, shallow breath, nostrils flared and once again reinforcing the image of a dragon. Dan took this pause to mean that it was his turn to speak. 'But Mum, I . . .'

'No, Daniel, I do not want to listen to your selfish excuses,' she continued and Dan knew then that she was on a mission and there would be no reasoning with her, he would just have to stand back and wait for her to run out of steam. As his mum persisted with the torrent of accusations and incriminations Dan's attention turned to the little figure stood beside her. Lottie was watching him, enjoying every moment of his discomfort. As she caught his eye she gave him a broad, malicious grin and then poked her tongue out at him. Dan looked up at his mother, willing her to look down at Lottie and see this blatant evidence of her trickery. But his mother was on a roll and nothing short of a miracle was going to stop her in her tracks. Just as Dan was feeling that things could not possibly get any worse, they did. The back door was pushed open and in walked Dan's father.

'What on earth is going on in here? I could hear the commotion half way down the garden!' Mr Jackson was a tall, severe looking middle-aged man with a neat moustache and receding hairline. He slowly looked round the room taking in all the evidence: Mrs Jackson had finally stopped shouting but still looked extremely harassed; Lottie had managed to turn on the waterworks and was once again sobbing hysterically; and Dan stood in front of them all looking like the accused in a courtroom drama. Dan's father's gaze rested on him. 'And what have we been up to this time, young man?' he asked. Dan remained silent, guessing that this was one of those times that an answer wasn't really expected, or indeed wanted.

'I think it would be best,' continued his father, 'if you went up to your room while I discuss this matter with your mother.'

Glad to escape the tense atmosphere of the kitchen, Dan stamped out and ran up to his room, slamming the door behind him. He threw himself on to his bed and shoved his head under the pillow. Why did they always take Lottie's side? Why couldn't they see what she was really like? They didn't even want to listen to what had actually happened. How he had been trying to do his homework on the computer and how Lottie kept pressing all the keys. Dan felt that he had actually been quite patient with her, but when she turned the power off and lost all his work, well, that was the last straw. Maybe he should have called Mum and let her deal with it but Lottie would have found a way to blame him, so what was the point?

'Hey kid, what's up?'

Dan's thoughts were interrupted by the voice of a stranger somewhere within his room. Slowly, he moved the pillow and raised his head to look around. Nothing. He must have been imagining it.

'You kid, I'm talking to you, don't ya know it's impolite to ignore someone like that!' That time he was sure, there was definitely someone in the room talking to him. The disembodied voice was quite strange, it was fairly high, almost squeaky, and the accent was like that of an American gangster, Dan had watched *Bugsy Malone* a few times and recognised it immediately.

'Hey kid, over here,' Dan's gaze followed the sound of the voice and finally discovered its source. He stared at it unbelievingly and his jaw dropped open.

'Don't ya know it's rude to stare? Geez, they don't teach you too many manners round here, do they!'

'But you're a, you're a mouse,' mumbled Dan incredulously. There, standing confidently on his windowsill, was indeed a mouse, albeit a slightly larger than average mouse wearing a grey trilby hat and little black waistcoat, but very definitely, without doubt, a mouse.

'That's very observant of you, you're a smart kid.'

'Who are you and what are you doing here? How come you can talk? You're a mouse, mice can't talk.' Dan started voicing all the questions that were bouncing around inside his head, but before he could finish his little white visitor interrupted him.

'Hey, hey, one question at a time. Firstly, I'm your MGF.'

This time it was Dan's turn to interrupt, 'What's an MGF?'

'Mousy Godfather,' replied the mouse. Dan just looked at him a with half-mystified half-amused look on his face. 'OK, so it's not the greatest title in the world but hey, it's gotta be better than Fairy Godmother and that brings us nicely to your next question. I'm here to help you with your problems just like a fairy godmother but way, way cooler! Now, in order to do that you need to let me know how I can help you, so go ahead kid, spill.'

Despite his reservations and concerns that he might actually be going mad, Dan started to explain to the MGF what was bothering him. He began with what had just taken place in the kitchen, and was soon telling him all about how the addition of Lottie to the family had changed his life for the worse. How even when she was a small baby she managed to get him into trouble, like being sick all over his clean clothes when they were just about to go out. As she grew older, her cunning developed and soon she had their parents wrapped around her dainty little fingers, managing to implicate him in all her mischievous exploits while she always got away blamelessly.

When he had finished, he looked up to see the MGF scratching his furry chin and looking thoughtfully at him.

'Do you want I should take her out for you?' he asked. Dan looked at him puzzled.

'Take her out? Like a trip to the cinema or something?'

The mouse laughed and then looked at Dan, his expression becoming suddenly serious. 'No, I mean t a k e h e r o u t!' As he spoke the words he drew his finger slowly and purposely across his throat and with this one gesture Dan was in no doubt as to what he meant.

'Oh, good grief no! I mean, does it have to be quite so, um violent, after all she is my sister. I just want to teach her a lesson and stop her getting me into trouble all the time.' Dan looked at the MGF pleadingly.

'OK kid, hey I can understand that, in fact I admire it. After all, despite everything, family is family. It's the same with my kind, we make certain allowances for our relatives, the only trouble is that in my species that kinda includes every mouse I know and even some I don't! Leave it to me, I'll have to think about things and work something out, you'll be hearing from me soon.' With that, he clicked his claws and was gone.

That night, as Dan lay in his bed trying to sleep, thoughts of the day's extraordinary events ran through his mind. By now he had managed to convince himself that it was all just a dream. He had probably fallen asleep after throwing himself on his bed, it was the only logical explanation. A talking mouse indeed, how could he possibly believe that it had been real? He was disturbed from these thoughts by strange noises coming from Lottie's room across the hall. Quietly, he crept from his bed not wanting to disturb his parents. He opened Lottie's door and stepped inside her room.

There, sat on Lottie's bed, was a hideous monster. It had short hairy legs and thick scaly arms. Its face was covered in warts, with a large bulbous nose and beady mean-looking eyes. Although Dan had never seen a troll, he had read about them and was pretty sure that this was what he was looking at. As his eyes adjusted to the dim light radiating from the small lamp, he was able to see more and something about the creature puzzled him. It seemed to be wearing Lottie's nightdress and it had long blonde hair, which it wore in pigtails, just like Lottie. A sudden realisation hit Dan full force. 'Oh no!' he gasped.

'Hey kid,' came a voice from the bedside table. 'Well what do you think? Now your parents will see exactly what your sister's like.'

The Lottie Troll whimpered miserably. 'Danny, what's happening to me? I don't think I like Mr Mousy. Why are my legs all hairy?'

'You wants take a look at your face, missy,' retorted the MGF and passed her a small handmirror. Lottie took one look at herself and screamed. Dan threw himself across the room, landed on the bed and firmly held his hand over his sister's mouth. 'Lottie, please be quiet,' he begged, 'you're going to wake up Mum and Dad, you don't want them to see you looking like this, do you?' Lottie shook her head, tears rolling silently from her troll eyes.

'Please,' Dan implored the MGF, 'can't you change her back?'

'Hey kid,' replied the mouse, 'I thought this was what

you wanted.' Hearing this, Lottie looked in horror at her older brother. Dan reassuringly put his arm around her, trying to ignore the repulsive sensation of touching her grotesquely textured skin.

'She can't stay like this,' retorted Dan, 'what will my parents say?'

After much debating and indignation on the part of the MGF he finally agreed to reverse the curse that he had put on Lottie.

'But before I do,' he insisted, 'I want to have a word with little missy here.'

Dan watched as Lottie the Troll listened quietly to what the MGF was whispering in her pointy troll ear, nodding occasionally and trying to hold back her sniffles. When he had finished, the MGF spoke aloud, 'OK then, I think you and me have some understanding now?' Lottie nodded vigorously. 'You just lie right down now and when you wake up your pretty little face will be back to how nature intended, capish? You just remember what I told you and don't you going telling no one about this, they wouldn't believe you anyhows. Would probably lock you away, thinking you was mad!'

Lottie lay down and pulled her blankets tightly over her head as if trying to shut out the events that had just taken place. The MGF turned to Dan. 'I don't think you'll be getting too much more trouble from the little lady, so I guess my work here is done. Take care kid, and enjoy your new life!' With that, he once again disappeared.

The next morning at breakfast Dan waited nervously for Lottie to come downstairs. When she finally did, he was relieved to see that the MGF had kept his word and she was indeed 'back to how nature intended'. His parents were both sat at the table and welcomed Lottie with their usual enthusiasm.

'Good morning, princess,' their father chirped, 'and how was your sleepy-byes time?'

Dan stared at Lottie and Lottie glared back at him. 'Oh, Daddy,' she said, 'It was horrible, Dan was there and there was a big nasty mouse and. . .' Lottie stopped suddenly and looked down at her arms. She quickly hid them behind her back, but not before Dan had seen the scales that were starting to cover them. Lottie looked at Dan with horror and, pulling herself together, continued. 'It was a really nasty dream but Dan came in and comforted me and I think he's the bestest brother.'

As Dad and Mum looked at Dan approvingly, congratulating him on such a thoughtful and kind act, Lottie slowly pulled her arms forward and discreetly examined them for traces of scales; they had gone. Dan looked at Lottie and smiled smugly. He had a feeling that his Mousy Godfather had made sure that Lottie would regret it if she ever tried to cause trouble for Dan again!

Shadow of the Eagle

Lynne Lewis

Bryn heard them long before he could see them, the relentless, ever-onwards *thump*, *thump*, *thump* of their hobnailed sandalled feet as they marched down the long straight road. The unstoppable Romans were coming into Cornwall to garrison the newly built fort at Nanstallon, to spread their imperial power into the most south-westerly region of Britain.

'The Roman infantry and cavalry are being posted to our land,' Bryn's father, Aruns, the chief of their tribe, had informed his people, just a few short days before.

'We are a strong, fearless warrior race, Father. Why can't we drive the Romans out of Cornwall?' Bryn had wanted to know.

Aruns had shaken his head and sighed. 'You recently counted your tenth year, Bryn, and are growing quickly towards manhood. You must understand that if we fought the Romans, we would be challenging something as powerful and unstoppable as the tides of the sea. Any resistance on our part would result in our people being killed or sold into slavery, and our houses and crops burnt down. We must act wisely. The Eagle of Rome has cast its long shadow across our land, and we must learn to live in harmony with it.'

Straining his ears, Bryn could make out the sound of horses' hooves clattering upon the newly built road and the jingling of harness. So, the Romans had brought cavalry, just as Aruns had promised! Bryn grinned, high up in the branch of the tree he had climbed to get a good view of the approaching soldiers. He had never seen a Roman horse before, but he had heard they were far larger than the hardy chariot ponies his people bred out on the moors. Despite his feelings of hostility towards the Romans, he felt excited.

Soon, Bryn could see them approaching in the distance; the light flashing on their armour and the colourful plumes of their helmets fluttering in the breeze. The road cut straight cross the sloping land and was built in the Roman way, with large drainage ditches running either side of the road surface. The tree was far enough away for Bryn to feel confident he would not be spotted.

Leading the force was the Commander, tall and olive-skinned, his dark face sculptured into sternness and stamped with all the arrogance and pride that Bryn expected of a Roman leader. Bryn's eyes were quickly drawn to a boy riding proudly beside him on a pearl-white pony, with a tail and mane that sparkled like silver. Bryn guessed this was the Commander's son, for they looked alike, both black-haired and dark-eyed and every inch Roman aristocrats. The boy rode well, sitting easily in the saddle, as if he had been born to ride. Bryn guessed he must be around his own age. The horses were beautiful, long-legged and powerful, and they moved with a fluid grace he had never seen in his peoples' short, sturdy chariot ponies with their fast, trotting gait.

Suddenly, the Roman boy's eyes flew up and spotted Bryn. He spoke to his father who reined in his horse and called to one of his men. The man, a great, burly Roman legionary, ran to the tree and grabbed Bryn just as he was shinnying down in the hope of vanishing to safety across the fields. The brawny soldier quickly searched him and then dragged Bryn, who was struggling, across to the Commander, who was even more impressive and stern close up. 'I couldn't find a slingshot or stones, sir,' the soldier reported.

'Perhaps he dropped them. Were you going to fire stones at my troops, boy?' queried the Commander in a harsh, heavily accented voice.

Bryn looked insulted. 'No, I wanted to see the cavalry horses,' he protested hotly.

'I warn you, we deal harshly with those who attack our troops, but perhaps it was mere curiosity that brought you here. I'm sure you haven't seen anything like our highly trained horses before.'

Bryn shook his head and glowered sullenly at the Roman.

'A sturdy looking boy, flaxen-haired and blue-eyed,

wearing a golden torc at his throat. Do you think this might be a chieftain's son, Marcus?' asked the Commander of the boy on the white pony.

Marcus nodded. 'It seems likely,' he said, eyeing Bryn with undisguised curiosity.

'I am Bryn, son of Aruns, chief of this land,' said Bryn with dignity.

The Commander laughed. 'Well, son of Aruns, you shouldn't skulk around in trees, but meet us openly, in friendship. Convey a message to your father. Tell him to present himself at Nanstallon Fort in two days' time. We have much to discuss about the rulership of this area. If you accompany your father, Marcus will show you around the cavalry stables and we'll arrange a demonstration of horse training and javelin throwing.'

As he ran home, the Commander's words rang in his ears, 'Tell your father to present himself . . .' – it was nothing less than an order, thought Bryn angrily. The Romans are already commanding our lives! He felt furious by the time he reached his father's house, but he gave Aruns the Commander's message.

Bryn was wearing his richest tunic and cloak, brooches and torc, as he rode beside Aruns in his father's light-framed wickerwork chariot, past the massive earthwalls surrounding the fort and through a main gate that loomed mighty and large above them. The soldiers on guard saluted them and they were escorted to the Commander's house. Bryn fingered his strands of neatly braided wheat-coloured hair and the heavy torc gleaming at his neck, symbolising his high status in his tribe, as he looked about the richly furnished reception room. Nothing he saw made him feel easier about the Romans. The gaudy red, blue and yellow murals on the walls, the low cushioned dining couch and the lamps hanging on slender chains from a tall stand looked foreign and strange to his eyes. Rome might be the ruler of the world, but he didn't have to like it.

As the Commander walked into the room with Marcus, Bryn was proud to see that Aruns was much taller than the Roman. Emulating their fathers' formal greeting, Bryn took Marcus's wrist in a viselike grip, which Marcus returned with the same bruising force. The two boys regarded one another warily.

Following a prompting glance from his father, Marcus enquired politely, 'Would you like to see the stables, Bryn?' Despite his deep mistrust, Bryn found the idea deeply thrilling, but quickly masked his excitement. He gave a sullen nod.

'This way!' said Marcus, escorting him out across the compound, past a large barrack block towards a long narrow building. Entering the stable block, Bryn could see each horse had a separate stall. The first horse was the purest black, with a coat that shimmered like jet.

'That is Janus, my father's horse,' said Marcus proudly. 'Only my father can ride him. All the cavalry horses are as wild as the wind before they are tamed and trained. We like our horses to have spirit, for they must be fighters, like ourselves.'

A pearl-white pony whinnied a greeting to Marcus and nuzzled his head against the Roman boy's arm. Marcus laughed and gave the pony a piece of bread he had brought in his tunic. 'This is Storm,' he said, 'and he is greedy for treats.'

Bryn didn't want to show how impressed he was by the horses. He decided he would teach Marcus that he was no belly-crawling Roman-lover.

'I bet I could outride you on a horse! We could have a race across the moors,' Bryn said, his blue eyes challenging the Roman boy.

Marcus frowned. 'My father said you were our guests and to treat you with every courtesy, but he did not give permission to leave the fort.'

'Perhaps you're afraid I'll beat you, Roman!' Bryn's voice dripped scorn and Marcus flushed angrily.

'I'd beat you any day, shepherd boy!' replied Marcus fiercely.

'Then prove it!' challenged Bryn.

Having saddled Storm and a chestnut pony belonging to a cavalry officer's son, Marcus and Bryn were soon riding out of the fort. While Bryn was unused to the Roman style of saddle, he had the advantage of knowing every inch of the land, but Marcus proved himself a superb rider and the boys were well matched as they chased each other across open moorland in a wild, headlong gallop.

Bryn saw it would be hard to beat the Roman boy and he desperately wanted to bring him down a peg or two. Marcus was too proud, too sure of himself, and Bryn deeply resented him and all Romans.

And then he hit on an idea. They were only a short ride from Redmoor, where there was an ancient, long-abandoned tin mine. The Spriggans, a faery race his people called the *pobel vean* (the little people), lived in the dark, cold depths of the mine. They sometimes played tricks on humans who ventured below ground into their eerie, shadowy caverns. It was just the place to impress Marcus with the ancient, mysterious power of the Cornish land. If he lured the Roman into the depths of the mine and left him there alone in the dark for an hour or two with only the Spriggans for company, he felt sure Marcus would be so gripped by terror, he wouldn't feel so high and mighty.

As they reached the mine entrance, Bryn motioned to Marcus to rein in.

'This is an entrance to the otherworld. Only the bravest of our people will venture inside, but I'm sure it would be an easy thing for a brave Roman to do,' mocked Bryn.

'I'm not sure,' said Marcus doubtfully. 'My father doesn't know we are here, and such places can be dangerous.'

'So you are afraid!' scoffed Bryn.

Marcus's face darkened. 'I'm afraid of nothing!'

Bryn smiled. 'Then prove it. The mines are haunted by Spriggans, the spirits of the rocks, so I would understand if you were too afraid to go inside.'

'Monsters, spirits and spells! Why should I fear them?' Marcus retorted hotly. 'I'm not a coward!'

From a small leather pouch, Bryn drew out his fire-making stones, flint and glittering pyrite and, striking them together, called upon the spirits of fire to send him a spark. Soon, he had two blazing torches to take into the mine. Leaving their ponies tied at the entrance, the boys ventured down the long narrow tunnel, slippery with algae and moisture. The light of their torches cast huge grotesque shadows on the rock-hewn walls, as if the Spriggans watched them as they passed ever deeper, through a maze of tunnels. Bryn knew his way through the twisting passages, but to a stranger they all looked the same.

Just as they reached the heart of the mine, Bryn snatched at Marcus's torch, hoping to disappear down a side tunnel and leave the Roman in darkness, but Marcus was ready for him and the two boys struggled briefly. Bryn cried out as he slipped and landed heavily on the slimy, sloping ground. His own torch was extinguished in the fall and when he tried to move, a burning stab of pain shot up his leg.

Marcus was immediately at his side, and lowered the remaining torch carefully to the ground. 'It's no good,' said Bryn, gasping with pain as Marcus attempted to help him up. 'I think I've broken my leg.'

'Then I must get help,' said Marcus. Taking off his own cloak, he wrapped Bryn in it and added, picking up his torch again, 'I'll be as quick as I can.'

As he walked away, the darkness swallowed up Bryn, enfolding him in its eerie blackness. As he lay there, Bryn thought he heard whisperings in the tunnels and the sound of laughter. His heart hammered in his chest and cold sweat beaded his forehead. He was all alone with the Spriggans, just as he had wanted Marcus to be, but they were playing their tricks on him instead. He would die in the cold depths of the mine, far from his father and family.

Could Marcus find his way out through the twisting tunnels? And would he come back for him, even if he did? The pain, anxiety and coldness increased, and he lost consciousness.

When Bryn awoke, he realised with surprise that he was still alive. He heard a strong clear voice saying, 'He's over here,' and there was torchlight. He saw the concerned faces of the Roman Commander and Marcus, and then his father, Aruns, was by his side, holding him in his strong arms.

'His leg is broken,' confirmed the Roman Commander. 'We must carry him to the fort. It is nearer than your village.'

A few days later, the Romans attended a feast given in

their honour by a grateful Aruns and his people, at the wooden tribal hall in their village. Over the central hearthfire, a huge boar roasted on a spit. Later, after the feasting, there would be music and dancing. Marcus came to sit beside Bryn, who was resting back on a pile of soft fleeces, his leg in a splint. The Roman bone-setter had done a good job and the leg would mend as good as new.

Bryn was shamefaced. 'I'm sorry I tried to trick you. I wanted to frighten you, nothing more.'

Marcus smiled wrily. 'I knew you were testing my courage, challenging me to go down the mine. And I was ready for your tricks. But if I had acted more responsibly, as my father expects me to do, we would never have gone down there in the first place. It is natural to mistrust each other, Bryn. Our peoples are very different. But couldn't we begin again? I like this wild, strange land and I think we could be friends.'

Bryn smiled. 'I would like that, too. I owe you my life, Marcus. But, how did you find your way out of the mine?'

'I wandered around until I could see light in the roof of one of the tunnels. There had been a cave-in, and I was able to climb out.'

'I did not think you would forgive me. Your spirit is generous,' said Bryn. 'From this night onwards, the people of my tribe will no longer mistrust the Romans and our two peoples will live together in harmony and peace.'

Also available from Chrysalis Children's Books

Arthur: Railroad Arthur/ The Lone Arthur

The Book

Alan Coren's irresistible humour takes centre stage in these wonderfully fun wild west adventure story books. Contains two great adventures in one book!

The Author

Alan Coren is one of Britain's best-loved humourists. Coren writes a weekly column in *The Time*s and is a regular guest on Radio 4's *The News Quiz*. In addition to the Arthur series, Coren has also written numourous humour books for adults.

Ronnie and the High Rise

The Book

Another weird and wonderful Ronnie adventure from John Antrobus. When the local high rise block grows up into Magicland, what will happen to the tenants? Can Ronnie outwit the evil Mrs Briggs and the rotten Lord Mayor? Another exciting story with Ronnie and his chums...

The Author

John Antrobus is a well-known scriptwriter and humourist. His many credits include *The Goon Show*. In addition to the Ronnie books, Antrobus has written *Surviving Spike Milligan* (Robson) about his days working with Spike.

ISBN: 1 84458 007 5 £3.99 Paperback

Available from all good bookshops

ALSO AVAILABLE FROM CHRYSALIS CHILDREN'S BOOKS

RONNIE AND THE HAUNTED ROLLS ROYCE

THE BOOK

A funny and surreal tale from John Antrobus about an elderly Rolls Royce which turns out to be the home of a frightened ghost. Ronnie and his friend Ethel take the ghost on a holiday and all sorts of adventures begin....,

THE AUTHOR

John Antrobus is a well-known scriptwriter and humourist. His many credits include *The Goon Show*. In addition to the Ronnie books, Antrobus has written *Surviving Spike Milligan* (Robson) about his days working with Spike.

ISBN: 1 84458 009 1 £3.99 Paperback

Available from all good bookshops

Also available from Chrysalis Children's Books

Xtreme Adventure Inc:
Attack of the Jaguar

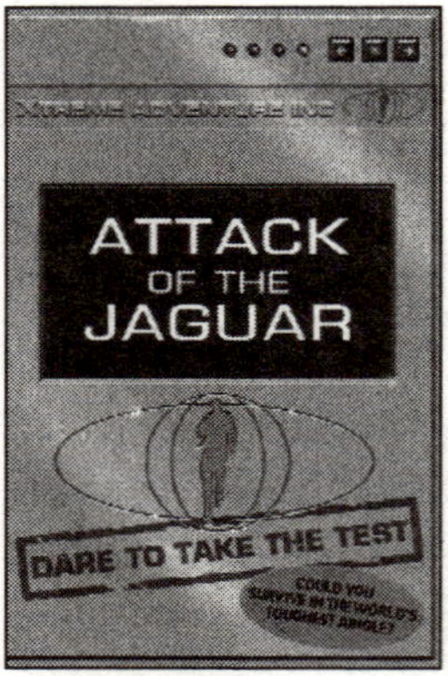

The Book

Do you have what it takes to survive in a dangerous, hostile situation? Xtreme Adventure Inc. is a secret world organisation dedicated to the good of the planet. Its Members have proved their bravery, brainpower and survival skills in frightening circumstances. Read their stories, take the tests, and see how you would have survived in the same situation.

Author Information

M.A. Harvey is a well-known author of fiction and non-fiction titles, including the *Who Am I?* series from Belitha Press.

ISBN: 1 84458 000 8 £3.99 Paperback

Available from all good bookshops